This book must be returned immediately
it is asked for by the Librarian, and in
any case by the last date stamped below.

Equilibrium and evolution

Equilibrium and evolution

An exploration of connecting principles in economics

Brian J. Loasby

Manchester University Press

Manchester and New York

Distributed exclusively in the USA and Canada by St. Martin's Press

Published by Manchester University Press
Oxford Road, Manchester M13 9PL, UK
and Room 400, 175 Fifth Avenue, New York, NY 10010, USA

Distributed exclusively in the USA and Canada
by St. Martin's Press, Inc., 175 Fifth Avenue, New York,
NY 10010, USA

A catalogue record for this book is available from the British Library

Library of Congress cataloging in publication data applied for

ISBN 0 7190 3488 4 hardback

Printed in Great Britain by
Billings Limited, Worcester

Contents

Preface

When I was invited to give the Manchester Special Lectures for 1989-90, the only specific term in the oral contract was that there should be two lectures, delivered on consecutive days. There was to be a modest, but unstated, fee; the dates were left open within a period of about six months; and the topic was not even mentioned.

Though this arrangement was perhaps an extreme case, it is common practice for economists to be hired on terms that are very vague. Yet the content of most economic theory is the analysis of contracts which are highly specific; and it is usually concluded – or sometimes assumed – that the absence of precise specification is likely to lead to inefficiency, or even a total failure of co-ordination. The organisation of the activities of economists appears to be at odds with the principles which economists prescribe for the efficient organisation of economic activities. I thought therefore that it might be worth using these lectures to reflect on what economists do, in relation to the phenomena which they purport to study.

It seemed obvious to me that I would need to go beyond orthodox concepts of rational choice equilibria, though I would need to offer some explanation for economists' use of rational choice models. But since I would be talking to economists – and indeed since I consider myself to be an economist – I did not want to abandon rationality in favour of such concepts as social pressures or psychological drives. I do not claim that these concepts are irrelevant, but I do not know how to use them effectively, and I certainly believe in the advantages of specialisation. Therefore my maintained hypothesis is that people have reasons for what they do. Often the reasons will be of the kind which later prompt the reflection that 'it seemed like a good idea at the time'; but then we should ask *why* it seemed like a good idea at the time. Only in that way can we learn from our mistakes, which can be the most effective way of learning.

In order to learn we must impose patterns on phenomena; that is the only way in which we can make sense of them. We may, of course, be making sense of what is not really sensible, especially when the subject of our study is human behaviour. So the assumption that human behaviour is based on reason, although a much weaker version of the standard economic assumption, can reasonably be criticised for assuming too much rationality. That is not, however, likely to be the response of most economists, and so I will not use any of my space to defend my use of that assumption; its justification must rest on the help it can provide to our understanding.

The issues to be discussed are the central economic problems of co-ordination and change. Co-ordination has come to be treated by economists as a problem of equilibrium; change, with which economists are often uncomfortable, is sometimes thought of as a problem of evolution. These concepts provided the title for my lectures, and a pair of connecting principles around which to organise them. I set out to explore the relationship between these concepts, and also the relationship between the pair of concepts and the problems of co-ordination and change to which they are applied. The latter relationship is rather easily extended to a comparison between the behaviour of economic agents and that of the professional economists who attempt to analyse that behaviour; and my one explicit debt to psychology – or rather to a particular psychologist – is to treat both groups on equal terms, as scientists.

This book has been developed from the lectures. Parts of it, especially in Chapter 1, reproduce fairly closely what I told my audience in Manchester, and parts of the remainder have been tried out on other audiences. I have attempted to use their responses to improve my understanding and presentation, as well as drawing on the ideas of, and discussions with, many people, not all of them economists. Readers who are familiar with Stan Metcalfe's work on technology strategy and the selection environment (e.g. Metcalfe and Boden, 1990) will recognise many similarities of treatment.

Finally, I must record my gratitude to Jackie Wright, who has coped with a succession of changes, large and small, in the text, as well as the many other demands of a productive department, amid the complete replacement of the University's word-processing system, and emerged smiling.

1

Economic theory and economic problems

Attempting the impossible

Economics is a very curious subject. If we reflect upon the questions which are investigated and those which are evaded, the factors which are carefully specified and those which are ignored, the methods which are favoured and those which are rejected, or even despised, we may well think that some of the selections are bizarre – especially for a discipline whose members often pride themselves on their devotion to the logic of rational choice. For the rational choices that economists attribute to economic agents exhibit no signs of purposeful reasoning; they are programmed responses to the circumstances in which those agents are placed, especially – but by no means only – when agents are located in a competitive economy which excludes every kind of competitive action. Economists themselves, having warned us to ignore what people say and take note only of what they do, rely predominantly for their evidence on published statistics and accounts, which as any sensible person should know are records of what particular people have chosen to say about what they (or others) have done.

I do not intend to criticise such practices in this book, though I do wish to point out some of their opportunity costs. I shall offer a few suggestions towards their explanation; but what I wish to emphasise at the outset is that were they to be replaced by another set of practices which some economists might like better, economics would nevertheless remain a very curious subject, with a different set of opportunity costs. That is because of the kind of subject it is, and the kind of creatures that human beings are. As I have previously pointed out (Loasby, 1989, p. vi): 'the economist's task is impossible. The complexity of the systems to be studied, and the interdependencies, not merely of its natural elements but also of human choices, are far beyond the bounds of human rationality. Yet we have both a psychological and a practical need to understand, and where possible to predict, the behaviour of these systems.' We should not be surprised that determined and ingenious attempts to do the impossible are apt to produce some very odd results; nor that, as George Shackle has observed, the life of any great economist, seen from within, appears as a series of defeats. Economists, especially economic theorists, deserve more sympathy than their critics have often been prepared to extend to them. But once we accept that economics is impossible, we can begin to understand it – and even to enjoy it.

I would like to direct readers' attention to a basic similarity between the problems faced by economists and by the economic agents whom they attempt to study. Both sets of people are trying to make sense of the world in which they find themselves, and to behave intelligently in it. (Similar parallels between practitioners of a discipline and their subjects may be found in other human sciences.) So the behaviour of economists may help us to understand the behaviour of economic agents, and vice versa. I propose to discuss both. In this chapter the emphasis will be on economists, and in later chapters on the economy, but I shall be particularly concerned throughout with the inter-relations between the two. For that purpose, I need a way of examining this behaviour which will help us to exploit these similarities; and the logic of rational choice, as that has been developed within economic theory, is not quite right, because it seeks to analyse behaviour on the assumption that we have already made sense of the world, and therefore know how to behave not merely sensibly, but optimally.

Perhaps some economists do indeed believe this. I don't; and I am pretty certain that any such belief must be false – for two reasons. The first has been recognised by Frank Hahn (1991, p. 47), who points out that the standard axiom of rationality 'may be *theoretically* as well as empirically unsatisfactory'. Even if problems are computable in finite time – which not all are – we should not forget that computational resources, like other resources, must be optimally allocated; but how are we to assess the potential benefits of those calculations which we have chosen not to perform? The very logic of rational choice requires rationality to be bounded. But optimal, or even sensible, behaviour requires more than rational procedures; it requires that they be applied to accurate perception. Economic agents are deemed to be in possession of all the data, and to have correctly modelled all the relationships, which they need in order to define precisely the set of feasible options which they face and the possible consequences of each option; and economists who propose to compute allocations are assumed to be similarly privileged. But there is no way of demonstrating that any such information sets are free from error; the 'sense' that we make of the world may turn out to be an illusion.

Reliable knowledge

I have a logical basis for this view, in the formal impossibility of discovering general truths by any process of induction. No matter how many instances we have discovered which conform to a proposed general rule, we can never be quite certain that the next instance which we come across will also conform to it. Infinite and instantaneous computation cannot overcome this logical impossibility. Perhaps there is indeed, as advocates of rational expectations theories are wont to assume, a correct model of the economy; but if there is, we can never know for sure that we have found it. It may be dangerous for either an economist or an economic agent to assume that we have. The recognition that a forecasting model may break down – even as a result of shocks which provide no basis for revising the model – may be thought to justify choices which do not flow directly from that model, but reflect the possibility that it may fail. Unpredictability is a kind of relevant knowledge which rational agents should use; to confine themselves to rational expectations, as these are conventionally defined, would be irrational. For if we expect the unexpected, we can do something to prepare for it. That we should indeed expect the unexpected, and that we can and should prepare for it, is a recurrent theme of this book.

Royal Dutch Shell has drawn precisely that conclusion. The trouble with using forecasting models is that they are sometimes correct; this encourages people to rely on them, and to take no precautions against the possibility that they may fail. It is to en-

courage their managers to take such precautions, and to prepare
for unpredictable opportunities, that Shell have replaced conven-
tional forecasts by a set of possible scenarios, to which they re-
fuse to attach probabilities (Loasby, 1990). They claim that this
policy has given them a competitive advantage. Perhaps their be-
haviour is worth some attention by economists.

If there is no way of establishing the truth of a general prop-
osition – and even the confidence limits calculated by econome-
tricians rely on the unprovable conjecture that the future will be
like the past – does that mean that we can believe anything?
Strictly, it does – and indeed, as we shall see, that freedom to be-
lieve is rather important; but it would usually not be sensible to
exercise it. Some beliefs, it seems reasonable to assert, are more
reliable than others. Indeed, at this point it is perhaps appropri-
ate to replace the label 'beliefs' with that of 'knowledge' – if
readers have been persuaded that 'knowledge' should not be
identified with unassailable truth. Much of what passed for
knowledge in previous centuries is now discarded; much of the
knowledge on which we now rely may be deleted from future
encyclopaedias. Nevertheless, it seems reasonable to treat some
knowledge as more reliable than other knowledge, and to do so,
in the first instance, on the basis of evidence. Even econometri-
cians' confidence measures may be relevant to such assessments.

Of course, not all evidence should count equally – economists
are right about that, even if the principles of selection which they
recommend are open to question. Karl Popper (1972) has empha-
sised that evidence supporting a proposition is especially persua-
sive when it arises from circumstances – perhaps deliberately
created – in which that proposition seemed most likely to fail; we
all know that it is often easy, by selective enquiry in favourable
circumstances, to come up with evidence which seems to confirm
very odd and unlikely propositions. Popper's principle, that one
should look for evidence which contradicts a proposition, is
based on the simple logical argument that, whereas any number
of supporting instances cannot prove that a proposition is always
true, a single contrary instance is perfectly sufficient to prove that
it is not.

But the logical truth of falsification is not easy to apply in
practice. The difficulties were illustrated by Alan Coddington
(1975, pp. 592-3) in pointing out that a theory in physics may be

falsified by experiment

only if the physicist is committed to a rejection rule which says that, in the event of a conflict between observations and predictions, the blame will *not* be placed on the observer, the equipment, the data, the calculations, the theories on the basis of which the equipment is designed, the theories on the basis of which the data were interpreted, the unspecified background knowledge which has guided the investigation or the concepts in terms of which the theory is expressed.

Coddington's list is not complete; in an interdependent universe no such list can be completed. It is impossible to test any proposition without assuming – usually unawares – the validity of a great many other propositions, each of which is forever open to challenge. Remember, there is *no* method of proving *any* proposition (other than a purely logical relationship) to be true; it follows therefore that, by Popper's own logic of falsification, there is no practical method of proving any proposition false. By demonstrating an inconsistency we can prove that *something* must be wrong, but we cannot identify precisely what.

This fundamental difficulty, which is usually labelled the Duhem-Quine problem (after a French physicist and an American philosopher) is well known to Popper, and much of his work has been concerned with the appraisal of conventions which may help us to cope with it. We shall be much concerned with such conventions and their consequences in this book. What must be recognised is that a refutation is not an event which a scientist observes – a theory overturned by the facts – but a choice which a scientist makes; and very often the choice is to reject the facts in order to preserve the theory. I argued in 1976 that this was often reasonable behaviour (Loasby, 1976, pp. 19–20), and was very encouraged when a distinguished physicist, Professor Ziman, shortly afterwards published a splendid book called, very appropriately, *Reliable Knowledge* (1978), in which he not only used similar arguments, but even illustrated some of them in identical ways.

Most of his book, I should say, went well beyond anything which I had written or thought of, and I have been very glad to learn from it. One of his arguments which I wish to use now is the importance of perceived interdependencies between propositions. In a well-developed science we may expect to find a dense network of inter-connected propositions about a set of phenomena, a network which provides reinforcement to every proposition within it. Scientists do not easily decide to reject a proposition if that entails significant damage to their network; it is much easier, and often more sensible, to reject the evidence (Ziman, 1978, pp. 39-40).

The importance of such networks offers an answer to the question that Mark Blaug failed to ask in his book on *The Methodology of Economics* (1980). He there accuses neoclassical economists, in one field after another, of failing to practice the falsificationism which some of them have declared to be their official creed; but he does not ask why they behave in this way. Interdependencies explain why. The belief (not always well-informed, in these days of specialisation) that similar ideas have proved very effective in other fields provides powerful reasons for sticking to them in one field where they may seem to be in conflict with evidence. If, for example, international trade theorists observe that rational choice equilibria are widely employed in consumer theory, industrial economics, analyses of labour markets, and macroeconomics, they will be encouraged to persist with similar kinds of models in spite of disappointments – and even though their observations of other parts of economics may barely extend beyond the titles of articles in the leading journals. I suggested earlier that it is sensible to treat knowledge as reliable when it is supported by evidence. I can now add that compatibility with other knowledge is another very important criterion of reliability.

Connecting principles

Networks, or clusters, of knowledge are particularly useful in coping with phenomena which threaten to escape far beyond the bounds of human rationality – which, I claimed earlier, is characteristic of economics. In slightly different language, I suggest that we try to make sense of the world by imposing patterns on it, and then sticking to them as long as they are tolerably successful in allowing us to feel that we understand what we observe and what we experience. This is not my idea, but Adam Smith's, in his account of 'the principles which guide and direct philosophical inquiries, illustrated by the history of astronomy' (1980). It is the central idea of this book.

Smith argued that people like to feel comfortable, and that they do not feel comfortable unless they can link together in their own minds the phenomena to which they are exposed. People prefer not to have to think; but what they like even less is the feeling that they do not understand, and in such a situation they are driven to seek an explanation. A satisfactory explanation is one that will somehow associate the disturbing phenomenon with what is already familiar, and thus restore a pattern of coherence. The motivation of science, therefore, according to Smith, is the psychological need to invent a set of connecting principles which will make sense of experience, and thereafter leave the brain in peace. It is 'one of those arts which address themselves to the imagination' (Smith, 1980, p. 46). The more extensive the range of a set of principles, of course, the better; and that, according to Smith, is why Newtonian physics, which connects cosmological with terrestrial phenomena, is so much better – for human psychology – than its predecessors.

I said that connecting principles are invented; that was Smith's view. He admired Newton greatly; but he was very clear about the nature of Newton's achievement. It was perhaps Smith's close friendship with David Hume, who had most clearly exposed the fallacy of induction, which allowed him to recognise that the marvellous congruence between Newtonian theory and an extraordinary range of phenomena, though of unparalleled power in persuading people that this was 'the greatest discovery ever made by man, the discovery of an immense chain of the most important and sublime truths', actually proved no such thing. Newton's theory was an invention of Newton's imagination, and might in due course be discarded, just like the invented systems which had preceded it, and which had been, in their time, accepted as true accounts (Smith, 1980, pp. 104-5).

It is possible to reconcile Smith's theory of scientific development with Popper's by treating each specific application of a connecting principle as a Popperian conjecture, which is then subjected to criticism and tests. Popper has never had much to say about the origins of conjectures, beyond his basic contention, shared with Hume, that they cannot be logically derived from evidence; so, despite his well-known antipathy to psychological theories of science, he might not object to Smith's account of the motives which produce them. What matters for him is how they are treated – and, of course, that there should be an unfailing supply. Smith explains the supply; and he also discusses the confrontation of connecting principles with the relevant evidence, clearly recognising the problems of interpretation which we now usually associate with Duhem and Quine. It therefore seems possible to combine Smith's theory with a realist epistemology, by which theories are neither instruments for prediction nor useful conventions but attempts to represent truth. Whether Smith himself would have accepted such a combination is a question we need not attempt to resolve.

What we may, however, note is that Smith's analysis of the history of astronomy anticipates the famous modern analysis of scientific progress by Thomas Kuhn (1962, 1970). Smith describes the extensions of each cosmological system to accommodate new phenomena (Kuhn's 'normal science'), a process which gradually leads to the accumulation of anomalies, or increasing complexity within the system; these difficulties progressively reduce its power to soothe the imagination, until some people begin to think that a different system is needed. Smith (1980, p. 46), like Kuhn, contrasts the 'tranquillity and composure' offered by a currently-accepted system (Kuhn's 'paradigm') with the labour and discomfort – especially the discomfort – experienced in the process of inventing a new system. In my view, Smith handles the process of paradigm change better than Kuhn, by showing the links between the stages of transition and the particular motives and concepts which inspire them. The discontinuities which Kuhn emphasises are obvious after the event, but they are the accumulated result of many smaller changes. This, as well as other aspects of Smith's analysis, we shall return to later.

The basic principles of Smith's theory were reinvented – quite independently – over two centuries later by George Shackle (1967), and applied to the development of economic thought in the inter-war years; indeed some of Shackle's sentences are astonishingly close paraphrases of Smith's (Loasby, 1989, pp. 1-4). Shackle adds his own ironical twist to the story: the search for the comfort of a more plausible set of connecting principles led to the disintegration of what he calls the Great Theory of the early twentieth century. What he does not add, but notes in the preface to the second edition (1983), is that the consequent discomfort provided the strongest possible incentive for the invention of a better set of connecting principles in order to impose coherence on the subject; and that is the key to the history of economics in the last forty years. Neither the creation nor the prestige of the Arrow-Debreu system can be understood without recognising its crucial contribution to the coherence of economic theory.

It is important not to misunderstand my comment on Arrow-Debreu. Anyone who acknowledges the fundamental impossibility of doing economics – which is a special case of the fundamental impossibility of discovering and comprehending the whole truth about the universe and our place in it – but also the urgent necessity of attempting the impossible, should recognise that I am not dismissing Arrow-Debreu as apologetics. The coherence of economic theory is highly desirable. It is important for our understanding of the economy, and it is important for the effective working of the economics profession – indeed for each individual economist, who requires some systematic method for coping with the Duhem-Quine problem to which I drew attention earlier. Very near the beginning of this chapter I observed that economists and economic agents faced similar problems in trying to make sense of the world, and in trying to behave intelligently in it. I now wish to point out the importance to both economists and economic agents of connecting principles, or coherence, in the first task and of co-ordinated activities in the second.

Co-ordination in economics

The co-ordination of economic activities, of course, is what economics is overwhelmingly about. In drawing attention to the importance of co-ordination in theoretical systems, I may appear to be following in the tradition of economic imperialism. Whereas Becker (1976) has asserted that the concept of rational choice equilibrium is the only proper basis for theory throughout the social sciences, I may appear to be claiming that the co-ordination of human activities (and, implicitly, the theoretical apparatus by which issues of co-ordination are to be handled) is the key question in all branches of human knowledge, and therefore that economists are uniquely qualified to annex an even larger territory. That, however, is not my position. What I am claiming – or, more modestly, suggesting – is that there are sufficient resemblances between the problems of co-ordinating activities and the problems of co-ordinating ideas – especially the problems of co-ordinating ideas within a loosely-organised discipline – to give scope for the application of a unified set of connecting principles to both. Indeed, in a fairly tentative way, that is what I am trying to do in this book. I do not, however, believe that the presently-dominant connecting principles of economics are quite right for that purpose, as I shall now try to explain.

The central issue of modern economics, to repeat, is the co-ordination of economic activities. Why do these activities need to be co-ordinated? The reason, of course, is that individual self-sufficiency is not usually thought to be a good idea. Adam Smith's (1976b) analysis of the causes of the wealth of nations begins with two propositions: first (p. 10), wealth depends fundamentally on productivity, and second (p. 13), the principal cause of increases in productivity is specialisation. That a suitable division of labour could lead to greater output was an old idea; but never before had it been elevated to the central principle of economics. Smith's formulation exemplifies his own theory of science, and the sequence of his exposition, which leads us from the image of the pin factory apparently set before our eyes to a more abstract contemplation of the world-wide flows of trade (Smith, 1976b, pp. 14-24) should remind us that he began his academic career by lecturing on rhetoric.

Now when people specialise, they become dependent on other people, not only for the amenities of life, but for their basic needs; so a failure to co-crdinate these specialised activities is liable to produce, not merely discomfort, but deprivation and even death – as we too often see on our television screens when co-ordination has collapsed. Adam Smith goes on to explain why a high degree of specialisation can best be co-ordinated by invoking self-interest. Smith did not underestimate the importance of friendship, or the moral sentiments which extended the scope of friendly acts; but 'in civilized society [man] stands at all times in need of the co-operation and assistance of great multitudes, while his whole life is scarce sufficient to gain the friendship of a few persons' (Smith, 1976b, p. 26). Where benevolence or sympathy cannot be relied on, appeals to self-interest are safer.

Co-ordination and the growth of knowledge

The co-ordination of economic activities, then, is necessary in order to enjoy the benefits which result from the division of labour. It is not a primary requirement, but a derived demand. Now that economists have begun to pay some attention to transactions costs, it is possible to enquire whether, or in what circumstances, these costs may outweigh the benefits of specialisation. The division of labour may be limited, not only by the extent of the market, but by the costs of the transactions which are necessary to support it. We should also enquire, of any system of co-ordination, whether it is well-fitted to encourage, rather than frustrate, the benefits which the division of labour offers. Now, of course, this is what economists do when they conduct their analyses of 'market failure', though they do not usually express themselves in this way. But if we ask *why* specialisation leads to increased productivity, we shall see that the orthodox analysis is not complete.

Smith (1976b, p. 17) offers three main reasons for improved productivity. The first and second are 'the increase of dexterity in every particular workman' and 'the saving of the time which is commonly lost in passing from one species of work to another'. Neither of these give any obvious trouble to conventional analysis, being capable of specification in production functions of a familiar static kind – though production functions which embody learning and the equilibria which they support may not be quickly attainable. But the third is not so readily assimilated: for this is 'the invention of a great number of machines which facilitate and abridge labour'; and invention, Smith makes clear, is to be thought of as a continuing process.

Thus the co-ordination of economic activities is not simply a derived demand resulting from a rational choice of specialisation in order to gain access to the well-specified benefits of a superior production function; it is a derived demand resulting from the attempt to create a superior system for generating new knowledge, the content of which, and therefore the benefits of which, cannot be known before it has been discovered. There is no reason to assume that the principles of efficient co-ordination that we have learnt to apply to the former will be appropriate to the latter. Indeed, my contention is that conventional methods of analysing economic co-ordination exclude any adequate treatment of Smith's connecting principle of economic progress. Smith (1976b, p. 21), however, draws attention to specialisation in the development of new knowledge by those who 'are often capable of combining together the powers of the most distant and dissimilar objects'; and this evocation of connecting principles as a source of innovation might encourage us to hope for some helpful similarities between the co-ordination of productive activities and the co-ordination of the growth of knowledge.

Alfred Marshall, who was even more concerned with the causes of economic progress, praised Smith's achievement in giving 'a new and larger significance to an old doctrine' (Marshall, 1920, p. 240). But he does not appear to have fully recognised its centrality. If he had, he would surely have made something more of his own ambitious proposal to link Smith's principle of the division of labour with Darwin's principle of evolution in 'the general rule, to which there are not many exceptions, that the development of the organism, whether social or physical, involves an increasing sub-division of functions between its separate parts on the one hand, and on the other a more intimate connection between them' (Marshall, 1920, p. 241). In thus propounding 'a fundamental unity of action between the laws of nature in the physical and in the moral world', Marshall offered an improvement on Smith's connecting principle which might be compared with Newton's improvement on his predecessors; for while Newton, as we noted earlier, brought terrestrial and cosmological phenomena within a single theoretical scheme, Marshall linked the previously separate domains of economic organisation and biological evolution. Smith would surely have admired this invention of Marshall's imagination as an exemplar of his own theory of scientific development.

Yet Marshall was much less successful in developing his connecting principles, which proved far less persuasive. Let me suggest two reasons why. The first is a simple question of technique: the analytical methods introduced to economics by Cournot, and adopted by Marshall, were ill-suited to evolutionary processes. The second reason is conceptual, and deserves a little more attention. Smith's principle of increased productivity through the division of labour embraced discovery and invention; and Darwinian evolution depended on the emergence of new species.

Both were open systems, and Marshall's combination of the two was similarly open: the current pattern of economic organisation, like the natural world, was the consequence of a process of innovation and selection, and provided the setting in which that process continued.

Now it was the openness of Darwin's system that proved most difficult for his contemporaries to accept. The idea of evolution was not itself new, and was indeed familiar in the context of movement towards a particular goal. Whig and Marxian theories of history, for example, share this form. But Darwin removed the goal. He sought to explain the origin of species, but denied them a destination, and therefore any ultimate purpose. Nevertheless, although many details of Darwin's theoretical structure have been questioned, evolutionary biology has remained an open system. Economics has not. Newton's model, in the form of the allocation problem clearly stated by Jevons (1871, p. 255), and discussed in the following chapter, has prevailed, and the system is closed in order that equilibrium may be defined.

For Marshall, however, the principal requirement of any method of co-ordinating activities was that it should promote development – the emergence of novelty. How are we to co-ordinate the generation and testing of new conjectures? That is not the question that is usually posed in the introduction to economics textbooks, or in the articles which predominate in the leading journals. It is, however, the question which has to be asked if we direct our attention, not to the economy, but to the economics profession – and to every other scientific or quasi-scientific discipline. Thus, while I am prepared to argue that Marshall's general rule encompasses both economic systems and communities of scholars, I am not prepared to argue that orthodox economists would make good colonists of this new territory. Their expertise is in handling well-defined problems, barricaded against novelty.

A concept of equilibrium

On the other hand, I do not believe that economic ideas and concepts are irrelevant, or I would not have dared to discuss these topics. It may help us to judge the problems and possibilities if we make use of Frank Hahn's proposal to shift the focus of equilibrium from prices and quantities to ideas and actions. I will not attempt to present Hahn's argument, or his supporting definitions, but come straight to his proposition that 'an economy is in equilibrium when it generates messages which do not cause agents to change the theories which they hold or the policies which they pursue' (Hahn, 1973; 1984, p. 59).

Hahn's proposal offers a prospect of liberation from the apparent need for a pre-reconciliation of choice which has long worried thoughtful practitioners of general equilibrium analysis – beginning with Walras himself. As Hahn (1973; 1984, p. 60) suggests, equilibrium may be preserved even if some markets do not clear, for there is no reason why rational agents should not hold theories which allow for temporary disparities between supply and demand, and employ policies which allow for quantity-adjustment in certain circumstances – as, for example, Marshall (1920, pp. 374-5) expected many firms to do in response to a fall in demand that was expected to be temporary.

Hahn's definition of equilibrium appears, at first sight, to be a formal paraphrase of that proposed by Hayek more than thirty-five years earlier; but it differs in a potentially interesting way. Hayek's (1937, p. 36) definition requires 'that every person's plan is based on the expectation of just those actions of other people which those other people intend to perform, and that all these plans are based on the expectation of the same set of external facts'; an economy moves towards equilibrium if people revise their expectations, and therefore their plans, in an appropriate way. Hahn chooses to focus on the theories and policies which generate such revisions; his equilibrium is defined at a higher level of the system. However, Hahn's characteristic insistence on precision leads him to define both theory and policy as fully-programmed procedures: a Bayesian updating rule for forecasting (1973; 1984, p. 55), and a mapping from messages to acts (1973; 1984, p. 56). Thus a succession of Hayekian equilibria can be contained within a single Hahn equilibrium – but only if this succession could be described by structurally stable equations. Hayek would not be happy with this restriction; and we will consider it again in Chapter 3.

Hahn's ambitions for his formulation are remarkably modest. He does not propose to investigate how agents might improve their theories and policies, or even how they might react to unexpected data; on the contrary, he advises us that equilibrium marks the boundary of economics (Hahn, 1973; 1984, p. 67). However, we can violate this boundary if we choose, and at our own risk. (We shall consider later the relationship between boundaries and co-ordination.) Hahn unconsciously invites us to trespass by requiring the agent's theory to be 'simple enough to be intellectually and computationally feasible for him' (1973; 1984, p. 58), and to be abandoned 'when it is sufficiently and systematically falsified' (1973; 1984, p. 59); these sensible suggestions seem to imply a continuing process in which agents interpret and react to events in a consistent way which does not depend on the pre-specification of contingencies or on any optimising procedure.

Equilibrium then depends not primarily on prices, but on expectations, information systems, and the interpretative frameworks which are used by economic agents. Intelligent behaviour must now include the periodic replacement of theories; however, it is still reasonable to enquire what forces hold theories and policies in place, if only for a time – in other words, how is equilibrium maintained? By a simple amendment to Hahn's proposal, to be suggested in Chapter 3, I hope to explain how the maintenance of equilibrium can facilitate the evolution of knowledge.

Given the problems of establishing the reliability of knowledge, which I tried to indicate earlier, there are no simple efficiency criteria which can be applied to a Hahn equilibrium, or to its persistence over time. What Hahn's formulation does do, however, is to focus attention on precisely those questions which I raised at the outset: how to make sense of the world – for which we need theory – and how to act sensibly – for which we need policy; and it does so in a way which might encourage a few devoted neoclassical economists to venture with me into forbidden territory. However, such an expedition requires more preparation, and will not be undertaken until Chapter 3. In the remainder of this chapter, I shall consider more conventional uses of equilibrium.

Equilibrium and closure

As we have seen, Adam Smith's explanation of economic progress linked development and co-ordination. Though he certainly used a concept of equilibrium, both development and co-ordination resulted from competitive processes (Richardson, 1975). Marshall associated development with evolution and co-ordination with equilibrium, and attempted to incorporate both equilibrium and evolution within a single body of analysis; but he failed. He hoped that his 'principle of continuity' would allow him to combine incremental novelty in an open system with the application of differential calculus while that system was provisionally assumed to be closed; but the general perception was of inexplicable hesitation in pursuing the logic of equilibrium – especially in his long-period analysis, where the strains, as he repeatedly acknowledged, were greatest.

Thereafter economists applied half of Smith's doctrine to their own profession, and specialised in the analysis of co-ordination, in the guise of equilibrium; they were duly rewarded with an impressive growth of knowledge. By a superb historical irony, the first major product of this strategy in Britain was Joan Robinson's *Economics of Imperfect Competition* (1933). (The story is examined in Loasby (1989, chapter 5).) Confining economic theory to the analysis of equilibrium greatly assisted the co-ordination of the profession; and the desirability of such a powerful connecting principle can be readily appreciated by comparing disciplines which possess one with those that do not.

That the equilibrium method required a closed system had notable advantages. It permitted an apparently unarguable definition of optimality, and promised great success for a policy of deriving system outcomes from a specification of system (nominally market) structure. Perfectly competitive structures had an especial appeal, for they allowed the principle of structural determinism to be carried down to the level of every individual. Perfect competition excludes all initiative; every agent is a prisoner of circumstance, and is unable to defy the economist's model. (No producer, for example, can avoid maximising profits, whatever his or her desires.) That is how we arrive at the paradoxes noted at the beginning of this chapter.

Now a world of universal perfect competition is almost as repellent as a world of perfect slavery; indeed the two are not easily distinguished. But for an economist, it has the supreme merit of predictability. Predictability is highly valued in all sciences, but it is of peculiar importance in a science which has taken co-ordination as its central issue. The more predictable is behaviour, the easier is co-ordination. If the economist's chief business is the analysis of co-ordination, the predictability of economic agents is greatly to be prized; and perfect competition implies perfect co-ordination. Indeed, as Demsetz (1988, p. 145) observes, '[i]ts appropriate name is perfect *decentralisation*'. That is why the paradoxes are so readily accepted, and why any suggestions that economic agents – managers, for example, or oligopolists – may have significant discretion are seen as requiring urgent theoretical attention.

Continuity and change

Unfortunately, if we squeeze out discretion, we squeeze out innovation. It may still be possible to have growth, through increased resources which can be used in ways which are already known; what we cannot have is economic development in the sense of Smith, Marshall, or Schumpeter – who defined it as 'such changes in economic life as are not forced on it from without but arise by its own initiative, from within' (Schumpeter, 1934, p. 63). As is well known, Schumpeter's view of change is one of creative destruction: new policies, based on new theories, destroy the equilibrium which rests on old policies and old theories. The new theories and policies, we should note, are not derived from data by any logical process, but arise from an entrepreneurial vision of imagined futures. For this process to work, it is obviously essential that the vision 'proves to be true'; but Schumpeter (1934, p. 85) denies the possibility of explaining how this can be. It is an assumption presented as a fact.

Yet Schumpeter is not an anti-equilibrium theorist; indeed, the key to Schumpeter's system is that the entrepreneur can formulate his new policy with confidence only when there is a stable, well-co-ordinated pattern of economic activities to generate the data that he needs to evaluate his vision and calculate his profit. When the entrepreneur destroys that pattern by his own innovation, he removes the basis of calculation which is essential if any other entrepreneur is to act (Schumpeter, 1934, pp. 235-6). Schumpeter's theory is not entirely satisfactory – we have already agreed that the economist's task is impossible – but it does warn us that zero predictability is no less destructive of enterprise than total predictability. That warning applies to the community of economists too.

Thus the relationship between equilibrium and evolution is complex. In many circumstances and in many ways equilibrium is an impediment to change; but in other circumstances and in other ways it is an enabling condition. Herbert Simon (1965, pp. 97-8) has made essentially this argument, that creativity is encouraged by an intermediate degree of structure. Kuhn's paradigms, by excluding fundamental issues, ensure sufficient compatibility of theory and policy among scientists to secure the efficient co-ordination of normal science. Paradigm crises loosen the structure, and allow people to entertain thoughts which were previously excluded – and indeed unnecessary to an incremental growth of knowledge; but it is never true that anything goes. Important themes and concepts are carried over, though rarely in unchanged form, as Smith shows us in his *History of Astronomy*; and the more striking apparent discontinuities within one discipline are likely to be associated with the importation of ideas from another.

Schumpeter himself tried to emphasise the discontinuity of innovation by remarking: 'Add successively as many mail coaches as you please, you will never get a railway thereby' (Schumpeter, 1934, p. 64). True enough; and yet, when the proprietors of the Liverpool and Manchester Railway decided to offer first-class travel, the accommodation which they provided was a set of mailcoach bodies mounted on a railway underframe. Furthermore, in combining the transport of passengers and mail, the mailcoach system of 1784 had introduced the practice of operating to a precise timetable. Indeed, any examination of railway development reveals its dependence on previous practice, such as the use of private Acts of Parliament by turnpike trusts and canal companies, methods of funding canals and the engineering techniques and management practices by which they were built, and the long history of waggonways both above and below ground. Change is linked to continuity, as is equilibrium to evolution. If, in Schumpeter's phrase, an innovation is a new combination, it is likely to be composed primarily of elements which are already known.

It is this linkage which explains why it is difficult to get agreement on the occurrence of revolutions in our subject. Is it helpful, for example, to talk about a marginal, or a Keynesian revolution?

Anyone examining either episode will note, first, that the theoretical structure changed substantially between the beginning and the end of the period, second, that these changes came about by a succession of steps, most of them fairly modest, so that discontinuities may be apparent only in retrospect, and third, that substantial elements persisted. By focusing on the first feature, one may claim a revolution; by focusing on the others, one may deny it. Moreover, since even people who agree on the record may reasonably differ about the weights to be assigned to the components of novelty and continuity, they may reasonably come to divergent conclusions.

The distinction between incremental and discontinuous change is an imposed distinction. All change involves at least one discontinuity; no change obliterates the past. The invention of such categories as revolutionary and normal science, or the hard core and protective belt of a research programme, like the familiar distinction between short- and long-run effects (which is also a distinction between degrees of possible change) is part of the process through which we try to make sense of the world by imposing manageable categories upon it. If driven hard, all such distinctions break down. Marshall, whose supply and demand analysis relied on them, nevertheless insisted on the pervasiveness of continuity, and inscribed in his *Principles* the motto *Natura non facit saltum* – there are no discontinuities in nature. Yet these are helpful distortions, when they are used with care; and I shall continue to use them – though not unquestioningly – throughout this book.

The organisation of economics

I shall attempt to discuss the process of change, and its interconnections with problems of co-ordination, in later chapters, making use of ideas from a range of sources and seeking to combine them into a few connecting principles; but I will conclude this chapter by briefly surveying some of the problems of co-ordinating the growth of knowledge in economics itself. For a survey which is both detailed and wide-ranging, and from a different perspective, I recommend Richard Whitley's book, *The Intellectual and Social Organisation of the Sciences* (1984).

An economist, to adapt Adam Smith's (1980, pp. 45-6) words,

'by representing the invisible chains which bind together all these disjointed objects, endeavours to introduce order into this chaos of jarring and discordant appearances, to allay this tumult of the imagination, and to restore it ... to that tone of tranquillity and composure, which is both most agreeable in itself, and most suitable to its nature'. Shackle's (1967, 1983, p. 286) equivalent statement runs as follows: 'All we can seek is consistency, coherence, order. The question for the scientist is what thought-scheme will best provide him with a sense of some permanence, repetitiveness and universality in the structure or texture of the scheme of things.' We need a theory which will impose order on the messages from our environment; and if it is our professional business to increase knowledge, we need a policy which will suggest how to set about it.

We look therefore for a set of connecting principles (Smith, 1980), an interpretative framework (Kelly, 1963), a paradigm (Kuhn, 1962, 1970) or a research programme (Lakatos, 1970), which will set our minds at rest, and encourage us to seek new examples of the applicability of our chosen scheme. Thereafter we expect to increase our ability to predict and control by incremental experimentation. We expect that any changes in the theories which we hold will take the form of modifications, primarily extensions; and we may decide in advance that no message from our environment will be allowed to displace any major elements. A very clear statement of the Chicago determination to preserve 'tranquillity and composure', while apparently extending its range, has been provided by Reder (1982).

Every advance of knowledge must, in the first instance, be private – as we acknowledge by attaching the names of individuals to new ideas; however, no advance is likely to have much effect unless it becomes public. Israel Kirzner's theme in *Competition and Entrepreneurship* (1973) is the way in which a market economy transforms private into public knowledge, and thereby allows that economy to evolve towards the kind of equilibrium that is modelled in orthodox economics. Kirzner's entrepreneur – who is very different from Schumpeter's – is alert to messages from the economy which signal some failure of co-ordination, and therefore (as in orthodox theory) potential gains from trade; his attempts to secure these gains – in Kirzner's basic case, by simple arbitrage – generate further messages, which cause others to revise their own theories in the appropriate way. I shall not try to appraise Kirzner's theory here. (That the prospect of gains from trade is sufficient to ensure that perceptions are usually correct is perhaps not quite as obvious as he believes.) But it is at least common ground that the growth of knowledge can be encouraged by providing incentives to individuals both to develop and to disclose new ideas.

These incentives may be influenced by the organisation of individuals in the same field. The process of improving knowledge by conjecture, testing, and criticism, is likely to be most efficiently organised in a structure which combines differentiation and integration, in accordance with Marshall's 'general rule'. This integration must include a set of conventions for coping with the Duhem-Quine problem, thus protecting the equilibrium which is defined by the current paradigm, or, in Lakatos's terminology, the hard-core theory and the policy prescriptions of the positive heuristic. Loyalty to these conventions leads members of the group, in Hirschman's (1970) terminology, to prefer voice to exit.

However, even economists who accept a common set of principles and methods are likely to differ somewhat in their perceptions and skills – especially if we bear in mind the comments of Nelson and Winter (1982) on the difficulty of defining, or even articulating, many skills, and their propensity to drift over time as the result of particular patterns of experience – and so may interpret and apply the common theory and policy in somewhat different ways. Thus the interaction between economists is likely to improve the quality of criticism and tests. It also improves the generation of hypotheses. As Marshall (1920, p. 271) put it in his own different context (to be considered in a later chapter), 'if one man starts a new idea, it is taken up by others and combined with suggestions of their own; and thus it becomes the source of further new ideas'.

The tendency to variation is indeed a chief cause of progress, as Marshall (1920, p. 355) claimed – and as Kuhn (1962, 1970, p. 186) repeated; yet this beneficial interaction requires a high degree of stability. People must already agree on a great many matters if they are to dispute fruitfully about a few; their activities must be co-ordinated. The invisible college must be in a kind of equilibrium; the messages it generates must not undermine the theories and policies which its members share. Yet if it is to be capable of novelty, the equilibrium must not be fully specified; there must be some freedom of manoeuvre, some unpredictability about what each of its members will do and say next. Given these apparently conflicting requirements, it is not surprising that we do not have very satisfactory general ideas about how to organise the growth of knowledge; and we should not expect too much help from the application of the dominant connecting principles of modern economics, which tie the equilibrium of a system to the equilibrium of each individual within it, and that equilibrium defined by rational, that is, fully-specified, choice. Hahn (1973; 1984, p. 55) insists that in his equilibrium no one is learning or discovering anything. He thereby makes even clearer than does Debreu's formulation that an economy in general equilibrium is intellectually dead – an unfortunate conclusion for someone whose own intellectual capacity is so formidable.

To talk to economists about the virtues of imprecision is to raise a spectre of jarring and discordant appearances; the response to such messages is often to turn up the jamming machines to full power. (That is one way of interpreting the assault on Keynes by those who insist that only fully rational expectations are intelligible.) Yet if we believe that economic theory has improved, we might recognise that the process of improvement has taken great advantage of the ambiguity and imprecision of language – the changing associations of the word 'competition' from active rivalry in Smith to a tightly constrained equilibrium in modern theory is an outstanding example – and also of the ambiguity and imprecision of the *applicability* of mathematics.

Herbert Simon (1982, 2, p. 399) has argued that if activities are to be co-ordinated, it may be 'more important, in some circumstances, to have *agreement* on the facts than to be certain that what is agreed upon is really fact'. He had in mind the co-ordination of activities within a business – to which we shall return in the following chapters; for co-ordination within a scientific community, especially one that is widely dispersed, we might modify his proposition to suggest that it is more important to have agreement on connecting principles than to be certain that they are the most appropriate. (I have in mind, for example, the principles which underlie the orthodox approach to problems of research and development.) Simon also draws attention (1982, 2, p.

391) to the 'social process of legitimation' by which supposed facts obtain their status; and that is a process which is always at work among economists, through books, articles, referees' reports, lectures, examiners' meetings, letters, staff seminars, discussions, and casual conversation.

These processes, especially if focused within a framework of connecting principles which is accepted as highly persuasive (as the formal rigour of optimisation usually is among economists) are very powerful instruments of co-ordination, even among people who have never met. They are reinforced by the language in which members of the group communicate, and the rhetorical forms in which such communications are set. They may nevertheless lead to error, in science or in business. But when they lead to success, the successes reinforce the appeal of those principles, and thus strengthen co-ordination. People rarely seek alternatives to a successful policy; indeed they rarely enquire about its possible limits. Equilibrium and evolution support each other.

The two worlds of economics

Since, however, the theories themselves specify what kinds of messages are legitimate (it is standard policy, for example, never to talk to economic agents, and hardly ever even to observe them in action; more fundamentally, it is never permissible to interpret any message as a report of other than rational choice), there is no guarantee that this well-co-ordinated activity will not drift away from the phenomena it purports to handle and thus gradually become less effective. Simon (1982, 2, p. 306) warns us that 'the decision-maker's ... perceived world is fantastically different from the real world', but fails to acknowledge that the urgency of agreeing upon facts – and still more, of maintaining an agreement once it has been reached – may accentuate these differences. Structural deficiencies in a model, for example, may be interpreted as errors in the specification of variables. (As we shall see later, well co-ordinated businesses can also lose touch with their environment.)

This drift may be accentuated by the tendency for any theoretical system to throw up problems which are internal to that system, and which often fascinate those who are most deeply committed to its use. As economists have increasingly come to accept – and indeed to extol – the concept of rational choice equilibrium as their most important connecting principle, it is not surprising that the internal coherence of the theoretical structure has become a major theme within economics – at the cost, perhaps, of appraising the coherence of an economy (for example, by assuming that all markets clear, without thinking to enquire into the conditions which make market-clearing possible).

Economists operate for much of the time in Popper's World 3 – the world of human ideas, to be distinguished from the material and mental worlds. But if the basic principles of their philosophical systems are treated, not as inventions of the imagination but as true axioms, then the pursuit of abstract rigour may easily be mistaken for an increase of understanding. This, I have no doubt, has been the principal psychological motivation behind the development of general equilibrium theory, the long rumbling dissatisfaction with Keynesian models, the devastating impact of the 'Lucas critique', and the acceptance by many opponents of the new classical macroeconomics that the expectations of economic agents must be specified as rational. In a brilliant but almost forgotten little book, Romney Robinson (1971, pp. 56-7) explains the hostility of Chicago economists to Chamberlin and Keynes in a similar way. Chamberlin's *Theory of Monopolistic Competition* (1933) and Keynes's *General Theory* (1936) portray levels of output, by the firm and the economy respectively, which are restricted by demand; and this reliance on demand constraints to limit the use of resources was perceived as a threat to the supremacy of the allocation problem in economic thought.

These pressures certainly help to co-ordinate the activities of economists; but since economic theory (to adapt Adam Smith's comment on Newton) is an invention of economists, not a description of the real chains which bind together economic phenomena, we should not assume that the internal problems of economics necessarily correspond with the problems of the economy. The applicability of any theory – not just in economics – is always problematic; the application of a piece of theory which has been tailored to an internal problem needs particular care. Such care is too often lacking. How many economists would emulate Marshall by visiting factories to see where Cournot had gone wrong?

I will content myself with a reference to a proposition which has been gratefully used to link positive and normative economics: that every competitive equilibrium is a Pareto optimum, and every Pareto optimum can be supported by a competitive equilibrium. The rather obvious difficulty in applying this elegant formulation is not just that neither Pareto optima nor competitive equilibria are likely to be attainable; it is that outside the world of the model they cannot even be defined. It is necessary to exclude large parts of reality in order to construct them; and how these parts are to be incorporated no one knows.

The commitment to Pareto optimality as the basis – apparently the only basis – for scientific welfare economics leads rather naturally to Samuelson's (1967, p. 39) well-known assessment: 'Increasing returns is the enemy of perfect competition. And therefore it is the enemy of the optimality conditions that perfect competition can ensure.' The assessment is correct; but why not reverse the order? The optimality conditions, and the perfect competition which can (in World 3) deliver them, are the enemy of increasing returns – and therefore of economic progress as understood by Smith and Marshall. The fascination with Pareto optimality and perfect competition is a major obstacle to understanding economic development. Yet this fascination is easy to understand as a connecting principle which both preserves the tranquillity of economists' imagination and co-ordinates their activities. The opportunity costs of abandoning it are rated highly by many economists. But these opportunity costs, I suggest, lie mainly in World 3; the costs of maintaining it lie mainly in World 1, and despite the ritual professions of concern for policy, most economists feel them less keenly.

As I said at the outset, I do not believe that we can eliminate defects of this kind from the study of economics; we may be able to reduce them, and we could certainly switch to a different set. It is not to advocate the abandonment of orthodox economics that I am now exploring alternative ways of organising at least part of the enterprise of economics, but to suggest a different perspective for other issues, to which economists could contribute more than they do at present. I believe that neither the conception of a general equilibrium of fully rational choosers nor the currently fashionable practice of seeking Nash equilibria for carefully defined games supply connecting principles which are adequate for our understanding of the problems of co-ordinating economic evolution. In the following chapters we will see whether we might be able to do better.

2

The organisation of knowledge

In the previous chapter I argued, quite conventionally, that the effective co-ordination of economic activities is necessary to secure the potential benefits of the division of labour, and – less conventionally – that prominent among these benefits are the generation of new products and new methods of production, which might require methods of co-ordination that are inadequately represented by the prevalent schemes of microeconomic equilibrium. I suggested, indeed, that the apparent deficiencies of Marshall's equilibrium analysis may be a consequence of his attempts to make it compatible with his emphasis on the importance of the division of labour as a source of new ideas. In this chapter I propose to shift the focus of attention from differentiation and integration as a system of knowledge production to knowledge itself. Among economists, that implies a shift from Adam Smith and Alfred Marshall to Carl Menger – though we shall return to Marshall later in the chapter.

Menger's theory of economic progress

Menger was a very different kind of thinker from either Smith or Marshall. Marshall followed his own prescription that '[t]he function ... of analysis and deduction in economics is not to forge a few long chains of reasoning, but to forge rightly many short chains and single connecting links' (Marshall, 1920, p. 773); but Menger's *Principles* (which like Marshall's, was intended to be Volume 1) was constructed as a single long chain, in which all major economic phenomena were derived from a single cause: human attempts to satisfy human needs. Menger, too, recognised the crucial importance of connecting principles, but (like his Austrian successors) he emphasised depth of structure rather than the breadth of coverage favoured by Smith and Marshall. This book favours breadth; it is therefore important to pay proper attention to Menger.

Human attempts to satisfy needs depend upon access to means of satisfaction; but, as Menger emphasises (1871 [1950], p. 52), they also depend on a knowledge of what means will serve – to take a primitive example, of what berries are nutritious rather than poisonous. In Menger's analysis, therefore – contrary to neoclassical theory – goods are not basic; there are no goods without knowledge, and knowledge is not to be presumed. (Since utility depends on knowledge as well as needs, it is doubly subjective.) Economic growth is then fostered by the growth of knowledge, the discovery of more and better means of satisfying human needs, for example by greater understanding of the effects of fertilisers (p. 70); this is Menger's theory of progress, clearly stated but not developed (p. 74). This focus leads Menger (pp. 55-8) to consider indirect means of satisfying needs, and his successors to the characteristic Austrian emphasis on capital structures. Austrian economists have continued to argue that the submergence of capital structures beneath convenient aggregates makes important issues inaccessible; by identifying Menger's starting-point we can see that such aggregation obliterates the patterns of knowledge which are embodied in such structures, and thereby frustrates the analysis of economic progress. As we shall see, this is true of aggregation both within and between individual firms.

Two other features of Menger's analysis deserve attention. First, not only is knowledge incomplete; it may also be false (p. 53). People may be wrong in identifying the means of satisfying their wants, and though someone who believes poisonous berries to be nutritious may soon discover the mistake (though perhaps too late for any personal benefit) other errors – especially about indirect means of satisfaction – may persist for much longer. At any time, there are likely to be many imaginary goods. Even if errors are continually being corrected, of course, the process may deserve attention – which it has received from Kirzner (1973). Indeed, as in a study of any branch of science, without examining the methods by which errors are corrected we cannot assess their reliability or their propensity to particular kinds of failure (Ziman, 1978).

Of particular interest may be the creation of imaginary capital goods. Hayek's (1931) theory of the business cycle was based on false knowledge, not about the properties of capital goods themselves, but of the equilibrium rate of interest. Excessive credit creation drives interest rates below the level which properly reflects intertemporal preferences; and by basing investment plans on these interest rates, business men create capital structures which are quite inappropriate to the real situation. They are structures of imaginary goods, destined to be abandoned. It has long been a puzzle to me why Hayek, whose concern with the problems of knowledge is now well recognised, never extended his theory to include the possibility of errors in the technology, or in the forecasts of future patterns of demand; as we look around, both seem to be rather more than possibilities. It is at this point that I see an obvious opportunity for contact with that version of the Keynes inheritance which emphasises unknowledge, as has been suggested by Lachmann (1986) and by O'Driscoll and Rizzo (1985).

The other important point to note about Menger's theoretical structure is his explicit reversal of Adam Smith's causal sequence. Menger (1871 [1950], pp. 71-4) criticised Smith for giving primary importance to the division of labour. Although he recognised Smith's argument that the division of labour facilitated the growth of knowledge, notably by the invention of mechanical aids to production, Menger insisted that knowledge also grew in many other ways, and preferred to think of the division of labour as one, very important, consequence of increased knowledge. Indeed he spelt out the sequence of increasingly indirect satisfaction of wants, based on increasingly complex knowledge: direct consumption; exchange for consumption; production for exchange; division of labour for efficient production. Increasing division of labour to take advantage of emergent knowledge is therefore a prime example of a productive opportunity, a core concept in the theory of the firm which is presented in Chapter 4.

Menger's conception of economic growth through increasing knowledge is very different from Jevons's (1871, p. 255) specification of what he called the 'great problem of Economy ... : *Given, a certain population, with various needs and powers of production, in possession of certain lands and other sources of material: required, the*

*mode of employing their labour so as to maximise the utility of the pro-
duce.'* Any attempt to explain changes in these initial conditions,
Jevons declares, 'is a total inversion of the problem'. Indeed it is;
but such an inversion is necessary for a theory of progress. From
Menger's viewpoint, as from Marshall's or Smith's, what Jevons
specified may be better defined as the 'small problem of Econ-
omy'. (In fairness to Jevons, it should be remembered that his
ambitions extended well beyond this problem, but were frus-
trated by his early death.) It is clearly desirable to make the most
of current opportunities, and Menger (1871 [1950], pp. 121-8) ex-
plains how this is to be done in language which is formally equi-
valent to that of Jevons; but in the long run what matters is to
enlarge the opportunity set by extending knowledge. That, of
course, is why Marshall was particularly uncomfortable with
Jevonian formulations in his analysis of long periods, in which
the supposedly 'given' was being changed by the long-run pro-
cesses themselves.

The scope for improving human welfare by securing Pareto
improvements (even including potential Pareto improvements)
in the allocation of resources is minute compared with the gains
through innovation. Moreover, the search for Pareto improve-
ments through the curbing of any possible kind of monopolistic
advantage may entail heavy losses in progress forgone, as
Schumpeter (1943) memorably argued. Optimal performance at
each point of time may impede performance over a period of
time. To accept that argument is not necessarily to accept Schum-
peter's theory of capitalist progress, which will not be systemati-
cally treated in this book. I will turn instead to more technical
considerations.

Coping with ignorance

Finding an optimum is a process by which one discovers a par-
ticular set of implications in the premises from which one starts;
and though the conclusions are logically contained in the
premises it may require much effort and ingenuity to discover
what they are. When supplying this effort and ingenuity it is
rather easy to forget that the premises themselves are always
problematic, and – even worse – may have been deliberately tai-
lored to the needs of the analysis. In particular, the specification

must be complete. That does not, of course, mean that knowledge must be assumed to be perfect; but it does mean that uncertainty is restricted to not knowing which of a set of possible states of the world is true (as for example, Arrow (1974, pp. 33-4) makes clear). Everyone is assumed to know that the set of states is complete, and each state is fully specified in all relevant respects. There is now a vast literature on the analysis of such uncertainty, with very little recognition that the specification applies to a very small proportion of important problems. Strictly, modern theories of knowledge tell us that it applies to none – but it sometimes seems reasonable to pretend that it does. That pretence, however, is likely to prove particularly dangerous when analysing decisions which are aimed at producing new knowledge, and thus adding possibilities which were previously not thought of.

The apparent power, and increasing accessibility, of formal analysis may not only help programmed activity to drive out non-programmed activity; it may induce the distortion of activity into a programmable form. Those who extol Lord Kelvin's dictum, that 'when you cannot measure it, ... your knowledge is of a meagre and unsatisfactory kind', might note Frank Knight's reported comment that when we can measure it, our knowledge is still meagre and unsatisfactory. Peter Drucker, who, over his long life has been the most consistently perceptive of all writers on management, warned in 1955 that profit-maximisation was most unlikely to produce maximum profits, because any formal profit-maximising model which could be used would be seriously defective. To achieve long-run profitability it is necessary to target specifically a range of factors which contribute to long-run profits, but in ways which we do not know how to model with any precision (Drucker, 1955, p. 59). Ten years later, in the first systematic treatment of corporate strategy, Ansoff (1965, p. 50) expounded a similar argument. It is not obvious that their advice is any less relevant now, either to productive businesses or to financial institutions. Indeed, the development of information systems, and the increasing attempts to base incentives on aspects of performance which can be measured, may make them even more pertinent. Management science, like economics, can operate in its own part of World 3.

The recommendations by Drucker and Ansoff may be linked

to a subsidiary theme in Menger's analysis, to which Hicks (1982, p. 288) has drawn attention, but which deserves far more emphasis. As I noted in the previous chapter, people are not helpless in the face of that very large component of uncertainty which escapes formal economic analysis; they can attempt to make provision against possibilities which can be envisaged only in general terms. Liquidity – uncommitted general purchasing power – is the only example of such provision which is sometimes admitted into economics, but as Hicks pointed out, Menger treated this as just one example of a large class, of varying degrees of specificity. Menger's (1871 [1950], p. 82) examples include fire extinguishers, which are highly specific, and medicine chests, which are much less so.

Many of our decisions, as producers or as consumers, are intended to create, augment, or protect, reserves or capabilities which can be deployed, offensively or defensively, in response to unforeseeable events. Ansoff (1965, pp. 54-9) includes the creation of these capabilities among the principal objectives of corporate strategy. No theory of the co-ordination of activities in the face of change can be adequate if it does not incorporate such behaviour. We might note two corollaries. First, since financial liquidity may be either a substitute for or a complement to other kinds of reserves, any theory of money which ignores them may be incomplete or even misleading; second (as Hicks insists) these are problems of an economy which is moving through time. The second corollary will be a recurrent concern, since an economy moving through time is the focus of our attention; the first we shall not consider further, though its potential relevance to the study of economic progress should not be overlooked. It may be worth giving a simple example. For many years, Arnold Weinstock chose to build up GEC's reserves against an uncertain technological future in the form of cash rather than by investing in the creation of technological capabilities of unknown value. This policy, one might suggest, appears more attractive in a financial environment where technology can often be bought by buying companies than in one where the market for corporate control is more tightly constrained; but it must be remembered that some, perhaps substantial, technological capability is likely to be needed in order to judge what companies are worth acquiring, and to make effective use of the acquisitions. As so often, substitutes are also in part complements.

People as scientists

If, like Menger, we consider the growth of knowledge to be the principal engine of economic progress, we should look for ways of building the development and use of knowledge into our analysis. As a bridge between the growth of knowledge and economic development, I propose to use the framework developed by George Kelly (1963). It is not irrelevant that Kelly's work was drawn to my attention by someone whose professional responsibility was the management of innovation, nor (as we shall see) that it has strong resemblances to Adam Smith's psychological theory of scientific progress. But it is most convenient to start with Kelly's objections, as a clinical psychologist, to the contemporary emphasis among psychologists on observation as the only valid evidence.

Psychologists, like economists, had been persuaded to become more scientific, and as part of the process to reject introspection and first-person explanations of behaviour. Kelly unconsciously echoes Dennis Robertson's (1952, p. 22) complaint about the long struggle to purify consumer theory: 'Was it worthwhile to go to such mountainous trouble to formalise in non-mental terms the behaviour of beings whom we have every reason to suppose to be equipped with minds?', and observes that psychologists make claims for their own motivation which they refuse to concede to the human subjects they study (Kelly, 1963, p. 5). (By endowing agents with rational expectations, economists, by contrast, grant these agents powers which are clearly superior to their own. In that respect the rational expectations research programme is certainly to be commended.) Kelly proposes to end this discrimination by treating people as scientists, and supports his proposal by a double argument about the enterprise of science and the business of living, in terms which I foreshadowed early in my first chapter. Let me indicate the elements of his argument which are most relevant to this book.

Kelly begins with an explicit assumption that the universe is real, and that we can have some success in understanding it. But because it is a single interconnected system there is no possibility of contriving a comprehensive representation. We must therefore create our own simplified patterns, each of which has limited applicability, and try to ignore the facts to which a particular pattern does not apply – perhaps compensating by creating other patterns with different applications. Because different interactions within the universe take different lengths of time to show themselves, patterns which work well over short periods may be misleading when applied to longer intervals – a quintessentially Marshallian proposition (Kelly, 1963, pp. 6-10).

Whatever patterns any one of us may presently be using, there are always alternatives available (p. 15). (It is not clear to me whether Kelly means 'in existence' or 'imaginable'.) These alternatives may differ, not only in their applicability, but in the appearance which they give to the facts (p. 26). (For an example from economics, we may note that whether a particular person without work is to be considered as 'involuntarily unemployed' is determined by the theory which we choose to apply.) Kelly apparently has in mind both different psychological theories and differences of interpretation between psychologists and their subjects – in which case the psychologist should not be privileged (pp. 76-7).

Kelly shares Adam Smith's conception of science as a fundamental human activity, which is motivated by a desire to predict and control at least some of the events in an otherwise incomprehensible (and therefore threatening) universe by imposing patterns upon them (p. 18); but he extends Smith's conception to include the use of connecting principles as a guide to action (p. 18). In Hahn's terminology, people (whether or not they are acting as professional scientists) use theories to interpret their environment and policies to decide how to act. Hahn, too, though he does not say so, is proposing to treat people as scientists.

Though Kelly certainly wishes to persuade psychologists to examine their own behaviour, and to adopt a new interpretative framework for their science, his principal objective is to develop that framework as a basis for a theory of personality which defines personality in terms of the personal constructs – the theories and policies – which an individual employs. His particular interest (and, in terms of his own theory, the motivation for creating this framework) is in psychological disorders, which are to be analysed by seeking to understand why an individual has been unable to develop serviceable constructs, and therefore, one might say, is unable effectively to co-ordinate his or her activities; but he recognises that a theory of co-ordination failure requires a prior theory of successful co-ordination. It is this linkage between knowledge and co-ordination problems which makes Kelly's ideas relevant to economists concerned with the corresponding issues in our subject.

In Kelly's phrase (1963, p. 7) 'the universe ... exists by happening': it generates a stream of events which are to be interpreted through the application of personal constructs. Some of these events are the consequences – not always intended – of policies derived from previous interpretations. 'Experience is made up of the successive construing of events. It is not constituted merely by the succession of events themselves' (p. 73). There are no facts without a theory – no unambiguous messages from the environment, in Hahn's terminology. (This is the viewpoint of Popper and his successors, as we saw in the first chapter.) On the other hand, theory can be influenced by facts; constructs may be modified in order to accommodate events which would otherwise appear anomalous.

Kelly allows for the refutation of hypotheses, though he recognises that falsification is a very complex practical issue. In seeking to explain why some people may be much readier than others to revise their theories and policies, and also what kinds of revisions are acceptable, he invokes the idea of a hierarchy of constructs, which resembles the concepts of paradigm and research programme, and serves the same theoretical purposes of channelling and constraining the development of ideas. Change is easier if continuity can be preserved. Indeed, this concept is crucial to his theory of personality: a superordinate construct which is permeable to new elements provides resilience, and therefore promotes stability (pp. 77-82); on the other hand a rigid system will prevent such adjustments despite the recognition of an increasing failure to predict and control (p. 9). A personality crisis, we might say, is a paradigm crisis.

In explaining Kelly's ideas, I have tried to suggest their possible relevance to the analysis of economic behaviour – although at the individual level their adoption would challenge some apparently impermeable constructs about the concepts of rationality, preference functions, and expectations. For me, a particular attraction is that they offer a basis for a theory of fallible co-ordination, which seems to me a serious deficiency in contemporary economics. In developing such a theory, it may be important to disaggregate the concept of permeability and investigate, in particular cases, what kinds of modifications are acceptable and what are not: the important differences, I suspect, are often of kind rather than degree. (That also applies to the development of economics itself – as one might expect.) There is, however, one limitation with Kelly's analysis as he presents it. It is intended, very appropriately, to be used by psychologists, and its emphasis is very clearly on the individual. Interactions with other people do occur, but their impact on the individual is all that matters. Economics, however, is a systems study.

The organisation of science

We can most conveniently overcome this limitation by returning to economics by way of science, which, as we have seen, was Kelly's model. Now science is necessarily a social activity; the scientific process of formulating, applying, testing and revising constructs is carried on within a group, and requires a substantial degree of co-ordination between members of the group as well as within the mind of each scientist. If the Duhem-Quine problem is to be resolved (or perhaps we should say evaded), scientists working on a particular class of problem must agree (perhaps tacitly and imprecisely) which parts of their constructs are to be treated as permeable, and what kinds of new elements are to be admissible. In Lakatos's (1970) language, they must agree on the set of propositions which are located in the protective belt, and therefore subject to replacement by others which will be equally effective in preserving the hard core, and on the positive heuristic which will guide – and restrict – the search for possible replacements.

The structures of science, like the construct-systems of individuals, are protected by their interdependencies; thus relieved of the need to preserve stability, the members of a scientific community can specialise on the generation of incremental change. A persuasive set of connecting principles is therefore a great aid to scientific progress (even though the progress may sometimes be in the wrong direction). Richard Whitley's (1984) analysis of the intellectual and social organisation of science uses this argument in reverse, by tracing out the impact of technical and strategic uncertainty – deficiencies in or disagreement about connecting principles – in hampering the effective organisation of the work of generating knowledge.

We must not forget, however, that alternative structures are imaginable, and that each structure is likely – even certain, as far as anything is certain – to have particular advantages and disadvantages. Different structures may be expected to generate different knowledge. To select a structure is to select – not entirely consciously – what problems can be tackled by what means, and also – usually with no great thought – what means will not be employed and what problems will be ignored. In Menger's framework, this is a decision about the creation and composition of the reserves in the system.

I would like to emphasise five aspects of the view of science which I have been summarily presenting here. First, although science is unmistakably a highly competitive activity – even if the competition is rarely as explicitly avowed as it has been by Jim Watson (1968) – this competition requires at least tacit agreement on a shared framework, which is not a natural given but a human construct. It cannot be a product of rational choice, but it can delimit the bounds within which choice can be rational.

Second, this competition is certainly not anonymous. It matters who is proposing a new idea, or reporting a new test result; and although reputations may be abused, or create innocently false impressions, it is right that it should matter. Moreover, this competition does not preclude collaboration, of varying degrees and duration, between people who are simultaneously rivals for fame and position.

Third, the framework, which, as I have said, is not a natural given but a human construct, must obviously be capable of novelty – of permitting the emergence of hypotheses which are not logically deducible from those already in the public domain. It is even too much to require that new hypotheses should be logically consistent with those already in the public domain. Kelly (1963, p. 83) makes this point about the succession of constructs within a single superordinate system, and Lakatos, as is well known, emphasises rivalry between hypotheses in the protective belt. However, Lakatos also insists on the maintenance of conformity with hard-core propositions, thus making a clear distinction between substitution and complementarity which economists should feel comfortable with – and perhaps even recognise the implications of. However, I have not found in Lakatos's work any precise specification of the hard core of any theory; and it is well known that the very concept of paradigm – which is an approximate equivalent of hard core – is ambiguous (Masterman, 1970). I do not think that this is accidental, though it may be unintended. It is a means of providing reserves against some potentially disruptive threats to our structures of knowledge.

Fourth, the concept of discontinuity, which is explicitly linked to paradigms, is likewise ambiguous; and that, I believe, is also no accident. It would take me too far from the argument of this chapter to develop the idea, introduced in chapter 1, that discontinuities are never absolute, and that important features survive revolutions, whether political or scientific; so I will content myself with the claim that the frameworks which appear to define a particular branch of science are necessarily imperfectly specified. (We can do a great deal while sticking to the idea of equilibrium – especially if the concept is assumed to include disequilibrium as well. That, of course, does not imply that we *should* stick to it.) Finally – a point which I take directly from Ziman – the quality of the results of science depend crucially on the process which produces them.

Marshall's theory of economic progress

It ought not to be a surprise to find that these five points are directly applicable to an economic system which is generating new knowledge. First, competition requires an orderly framework. Second, it should not be anonymous, nor exclude collaboration. Third, the framework should be imperfectly specified. Fourth, though there may be important discontinuities, major concepts and structures should adapt and persist. Fifth, the quality of the results depends on the process. That does not sound very like a characterisation of neoclassical economics. It is, however, a justifiable, if incomplete, characterisation of Marshall's analysis of firms and markets.

Alfred Marshall's reputation as a neoclassical economist rests primarily on Book V of his *Principles of Economics* (1920); and it is generally agreed – by those who are not familiar with what he actually wrote – that this reputation is flawed. As was pointed out by Sraffa (1926), and has been emphasised most notably by Samuelson (1967, p. 25), Book V does not contain a satisfactory model of perfect competition. But what neither Sraffa nor Samuelson recognised was that Marshall did not intend to develop a theory of perfect competition. He was not content to be confined by either the rules or the objectives of what we now call neoclassical economics; his concern was with human progress.

Book IV of Marshall's *Principles* is called 'The Agents of Production. Land, Labour, Capital and Organisation', and in the introductory chapter, after a brief definition of land, labour and capital, the second paragraph begins like this:

Capital consists in a great part of knowledge and organisation; and of this some part is private property and other part is not. Knowledge is our most powerful engine of production; it enables us to subdue Nature and force her to satisfy our wants. Organisation aids knowledge; it has many forms, e.g. that of a single business, that of various businesses in the same trade, that of various trades relatively to one another, and that of the State providing security for all and help for many. (Marshall, 1920, pp. 138-9)

Marshall has much to say, in the *Principles* and in *Industry and Trade* (1919), about the importance and implications of knowledge – including the implications for the attainability of equilibrium, a theme which I have developed elsewhere (1989, pp. 61-70) and of which I will here say only that Marshall's discussion is always related to the informational structures which are embedded in Marshallian markets – and which of course are incompatible with the requirements of perfect competition. What I now wish to concentrate on are the effects of organisation on the development and use of knowledge.

There is no evidence that Marshall's identification of knowledge as 'our most powerful engine of production' was derived from Menger. It is not possible to prove that there was no influence – none of us can be sure that we have not been influenced, even unconsciously, by anything that we have read – but it is easy to believe that Marshall invented this connecting principle (which, be it noted, makes no mention of knowledge in consumption – Menger's starting point) to impose order on his investigations into manufacturing technology and business management, which no other major economist has thought to emulate. His connection between knowledge and organisation, which is far clearer and stronger than anything that Menger said, is also readily interpreted as a construct imposed on those investigations.

However, Marshall failed to make use of these twin principles, which were added respectively to the third and fourth editions of the *Principles*, in the way that Menger, with his insistence on logical structures of argument, would surely have done. Not only does he make no attempt to discuss their relationship with his general rule of development through differentiation and integration (thereby ignoring Menger's argument for the logical priority of knowledge over the division of labour); he made no changes in the chapters on business management to bring their sequence of topics into alignment with his very convenient specification of forms of organisation. In relation to his own taxonomy, this sequence is very badly arranged, and its effectiveness is thereby reduced.

I have attempted a reconstruction of Marshall's analysis, using Marshall's own categories, in my contribution to the Royal Economic Society Centenary Volume on Marshall's *Principles* (Whitaker, 1990, pp. 108-26). Let me summarise the argument. Marshall's businessmen are expected to use their knowledge of their trade to experiment with both processes and products – and not only in response to demand but in anticipation of it; they are expected to build up an organisation – which takes time – that will combine specialisation and integration, and to encourage initiative in their subordinates. They make use of their own particular abilities and experience in their own particular circumstances, thus generating an approximate equivalent of Darwinian variation. That is Marshall's first form of organisation.

Where similar businesses are collected together in an industrial district, this district serves as an invisible college, in which ideas are exchanged and developed: conjecture, refutation, and also criticism – which, let us remember, is an essential part of the Popperian recipe – are encouraged. (Marshall did not ignore, though we can now see that he underestimated, the danger that the continuing contacts within an industrial district may eventually impart too much rigidity to the framework; outsiders might prosper by their exemption from conventional wisdom.) A dispersed industry constitutes a looser invisible college, linked by some personal contacts but also by its trade journals. That is the second form of organisation.

In addition to this pattern of competition and collaboration with similar businesses in the generation of new knowledge, firms are linked to suppliers and customers in a network of information and ideas – the third form of organisation – which, in the words of one of my students, provides an agenda for innovation. (The importance of such networks, especially for small businesses, I should report, is currently a fashionable idea in business studies, and among those who are introduced to it Marshall's analysis is well – and sometimes enthusiastically – received.) Marshall calls this network the firm's 'external organisation', thus substantially, and I am sure deliberately, blurring the contrast between the firm's internal arrangements and its market relationships, which we have been trained to emphasise; that is one of the themes of my centenary article.

Marshall emphasises – in so far as he ever emphasises anything – the importance of a firm's external organisation as part of its capital, which may even be of greater value than its tangible assets; the careful accumulation of this capital, and its subsequent erosion through inadequate attention to renewal, are major elements in his account of the firm's life-cycle. Such capital, of course, does not appear in the balance sheet (it would be very inadequately represented by the valuation of brand names which has recently been advocated); and it certainly is not suitable for aggregation. We may note, however, that it does match the Austrian emphasis on capital structures, though not the Austrian assumption that the relevant knowledge is embodied in physical plant.

There is another Austrian parallel implicit in Marshall's treatment. Though the firm's organisation, both internal and external, is specific to its particular business and situation, it is not specific to any particular plan. It defines – imprecisely, of course – a set of capabilities. It may appropriately be compared to Menger's conception of reserves which are provided against unpredictable events, especially if we recognise the value of such reserves in exploiting opportunities as well as in responding to threats. Menger, as we have noted, saw the deliberate creation of reserves as a general feature of intelligent human choice; in this particular context we may think primarily of opportunities revealed by the firm's contacts, and threats arising from new ideas and actions of its rivals. But Marshall implicitly extends Menger's conception to include the capabilities which are not under the control of an individual or single business, but which are distributed among the members of a group of businesses, whether rivals or collaborators – or often both.

Though Marshall's exposition is not well related to the connecting principles which are announced at the beginning of Book IV, it clearly displays the co-ordination of the growth of knowledge in the economy as a process employing a blend of competition and co-operation – which, as Marshall (1920, p. 5) had declared much earlier, are twin manifestations of enterprise. How closely this process resembles the co-ordination of the growth of knowledge in scientific communities, including the community of economists, has been so little remarked that I have chosen to give it some emphasis in this book. Marshall also shows us the process operating at different levels, and it is this feature that we shall examine in the following chapter.

3

Economic organisation

Coherence and change

In the first chapter, I argued that the conventional specification of the co-ordination problem, so central to economics, is a misrepresentation of the problem of co-ordinating activities in an economy which is developing, in Schumpeter's phrase, from within. The coherence of economic systems has come to be defined as a problem of the existence and stability (sometimes also the uniqueness) of equilibrium, and that has entailed the specification of a closed set of possibilities – and in the long-dominant case of perfect competition, a specification which allows economic agents to choose only quantities of commodities from a predetermined set. But the problem for a developing economy is that of maintaining coherence, first, in the face of many and varied changes – what might be called a turbulent environment – and second, while creating new possibilities – indeed in a way which will encourage their creation.

Progress in response to change, it might be claimed, can be handled by the method of comparative equilibrium; but I would dispute that claim on two grounds. First, comparative equilibrium methods do not indicate how, or even whether, an economy can make the necessary transition between equilibria; this difficulty is widely recognised, but not resolved. Indeed, Richardson (1960; 1990) has persuasively argued that the specification which allows economists to prove the formal existence of a perfectly competitive equilibrium is incapable of permitting rational adjustment, and is therefore a potentially misleading guide to policy. The difficulties are so formidable that many microeconomists appear to have forsaken the magnificent research programme of general equilibrium in favour of the local equilibria of semi-arbitrary games – a second disintegration of a coherent theory of value which may one day be compared with that so perceptively examined by Shackle (1967). Nash equilibria constrain each individual as tightly as perfect competition, and have the advantage that the discovery of such equilibria apparently requires neither an auctioneer nor any transactions which might disturb the outcome, but simply individual ratiocination. All actions are therefore equilibrium actions, as a rigorous insistence on optimisation demands. However, each Nash equilibrium requires all players to be smart enough to work out the implications of the rules of the game, but not smart enough to recognise the potential advantages of varying them (Simon, 1982, 2, p. 216). They are only boundedly rational after all.

My second objection is that the method of comparing equilibria before and after a change is not consistent with the definition of equilibrium which is used in rigorous theory. The method requires the change to be totally unforeseen; but it is quite improper to impose a shock on an Arrow-Debreu model, which requires *all* contingencies – all possible shocks – to be specified in setting up the model. The occurence of a contingency not previously specified would demonstrate that the economy had not been in a true Arrow-Debreu equilibrium at all. Indeed, it is not easy to reconcile the concept of a shock with a rigorous definition of rationality. It is not enough to require both the timing and the content of future shocks to be unpredictable, so that they provide no information which might improve any agent's forecasting model. A forecasting model which is known to be subject to unpredictable error should not be used as if it were a model which was known to forecast perfectly. Rational agents do not ignore the unexpected just because it is unpredictable, as I pointed out early in Chapter 1.

The analysis of change itself encounters a further level of difficulty. What purports to be the neoclassical analysis of research and development (which, by the rules of the neoclassical game, can hardly avoid exposing market failure) does not deal formally with the emergence of novelty; it is the analysis of a treasure hunt. Moreover, the organisation of this treasure hunt is discussed in relation to market structures; the management of the process does not receive much attention. This research programme within economics is largely driven by problems generated by the theoretical system employed – it belongs in World 3; and its analytical methods are rather obviously constrained by that system. That does not mean that its results are worthless; but it does mean that their applicability must be judged by external criteria. It does have, however, a potential use which is not widely recognised: as a case study in the co-ordination of activities which are intended to generate new knowledge by extending the scope of established methods. The preferred means of co-ordinating the activities of economists have been efficient in generating certain kinds of knowledge; but they have obstructed the development of other kinds, which might be more important. I suggest that something similar happens in many firms and in many industries; indeed I will provide some examples later.

Let us then see if we can find another way by which economists may attempt to handle this redefined problem of co-ordination without abandoning the concept of equilibrium. Unlike some other economists – notably some members of the Austrian school in the United States – I do not believe that we need to abandon equilibrium ideas – even though people seem to write effectively about the growth of knowledge without them. We must recognise at the outset that we shall not produce any models of perfect co-ordination to set alongside perfect competition; instead we may be able to produce theories of fallible co-ordination. As I remarked in the previous chapter, that does not disturb me in the least; the co-ordination of our economies is indeed fallible – not in the sense of market failure equilibrium, but in the simple sense that the means which are used sometimes work and sometimes don't. If economics is about co-ordination these are the central phenomena to explain.

Equilibrium and decomposability

Let us return to Frank Hahn's definition, and see what we might get out of that.

'An economy is in equilibrium when it generates messages which do not cause agents to change the theories which they hold or the policies which they pursue' (1973; 1984, p. 59). Each agent uses the relevant theory to interpret each message from the economy and thereby generates a forecast; for each forecast the agent's policy generates an appropriate action, which normally elicits a further message from the economy. Though forecasts and acts may change as messages change, equilibrium, in Hahn's sense, is preserved as long as each agent continues to follow the routines which are embedded in an unchanging set of theories and policies. Theories and policies thus operate in ways which could in principle be accurately modelled by an observer (Hahn, 1973; 1984, pp. 55-6) – who might, however, find it hard to distinguish between a human agent and a computer program.

Hahn's conception allows for variations in prices and quantities, and even for some excess demands and unemployed resources, since theories and policies may allow for frictions; but it excludes the slightest change in any agent's understanding of the world. On Hahn's definition, the generation of knowledge must lead to a change in at least one theory or policy; this makes the generation of knowledge incompatible with the preservation of equilibrium. That was precisely Schumpeter's (1934) view: indeed the destruction by new knowledge of a general equilibrium of routines which support a circular flow is the best-known feature of his theory of economic development. Thus, despite using the very relevant categories of theory and policy, Hahn's definition will not help us to think about co-ordinating a process of change – as it stands.

Hahn's system has three tightly-integrated levels: the economy, agents' theories and policies, and particular forecasts and acts (what Hayek called expectations and plans). The obvious move is to relax this integration, first, by decoupling the equilibrium of the economy from the equilibrium of every agent, and, second, by interpreting theories and policies, not as precisely-specified logical structures, but as research programmes which provide a framework to guide agents in formulating their expectations and plans. To do this is to return to an older tradition, exemplified by Marshall's equilibrium of an industry composed of ever-changing firms, whose last major defender, I believe, was Sir Dennis Robertson; its abandonment in the 1920s is a clear indication that theoretical coherence was gaining priority among economists over the co-ordination of activities in a real economy. For decoupling a system both from its environment and from each individual element among the many which constitute it is the classic method of stabilising that system, in biological populations, engineering systems, organisational structures, and in scientific disciplines.

Decoupling from the environment reduces the impact of external events; and if the impact cannot be avoided, then system coherence may be enhanced by reducing system integration, especially if the changes are hard to predict. Loose coupling is a means of providing reserves at the system level. It allows some of the elements to change, either in response to pressures of various kinds or by their own initiative, without disturbing the balance of the system to which they belong. Instead of seeking conditions which are capable of supporting a general equilibrium, we may do better to seek conditions which will make it unnecessary.

The concept of a decomposable system, in which higher-level equilibrium is both partly insulated from disequilibrium among its elements and provides some constraints – which are not very precise – upon the behaviour of those elements, also suggests a way of dealing with a serious problem in Hahn's model, to which he is not blind. This problem is simply this: what happens if an agent is persuaded that one or more of the current theories or policies needs replacing? Bayesian updating cannot provide an answer; for that, as Hahn (1973; 1984, p. 55) makes clear, is a process controlled by the agent's theoretical system, and cannot be used to replace it. Since this system, like other general equilibrium models, has no intermediate structure between individual agents and the total economy, any disturbance is liable to cause disintegration. Indeed, Hahn's equilibrium seems to describe very well Schumpeter's conception of an economy in which 'things have had time enough to hammer logic into men' (Schumpeter, 1934, p. 80), and which therefore exhibits an integrated set of efficient routines. Now Schumpeter argued that disturbances to this routine could not be expected to lead at all easily or quickly to the establishment of a satisfactory replacement; and Hahn's discussion gives us no reason to question that argument.

Contemporary theories of knowledge also warn us that the refutation of one conjecture does not carry with it a better alternative. However, although there can logically be no guaranteed method of generating conjectures, the acceptance of a continuing pattern, framework, paradigm, or research programme may be of great help in promoting the kind of association of ideas which seems so often to be involved in that process. We may therefore add another level to Hahn's system, a level in which agents have theories about the generation of theories, and policies for the formulation of policies. Such meta-theories and meta-policies cannot be precisely specified, because it is logically impossible for the content of new knowledge to be predicted in advance or, what comes to the same thing, to be specified as the output, determinate or probabilistic, of a well-defined process. That may be why, in 1973, Hahn placed the generation or revision of theories and policies beyond the scope of economic analysis. He now (1991) believes that we cannot deal adequately with some important problems without extending that scope, and recognises that such extensions imply substantial revisions of the theories and policies which economists use.

Decomposable systems

Herbert Simon (1969) argued twenty years ago that complex natural systems are likely to be highly decomposable. His basic reason is that complex systems have emerged, over the life of the universe, from simple elements, and that emergent complex systems which were not decomposable would have little prospect of surviving in an often turbulent environment. Simon associates decomposability with hierarchical structures, which is fine so long as we think not of integrated command systems but of devolution.

He goes on to argue that it is because complex systems are decomposable that they can be successfully studied piecemeal, in the way in which sciences have grown up. We can understand a great deal about animal cells without bothering much about either the animal to which they belong or the molecules which compose them; animal populations and elementary particles we may ignore entirely. Our ability to understand the world despite the bounds on our rationality, he suggests, is a consequence of the world being the way that it is; but that is the only way that it could be. (This, of course, is not to claim that the particular kinds of decomposable systems which we observe are the only kinds that could have evolved). A world which could be accurately represented by the kind of general equilibrium postulated by economists, in which there are no significant groupings of individuals below the level of a complete economic system, is, it appears, not a world with which human beings could cope. Simon's argument implies that if a tolerable degree of co-ordination is to be achieved, any equilibrium representation of such co-ordination should rely on a set of partial equilibria.

Let me make four observations on Simon's argument. The first, which is taken from Simon, is a direct consequence of bounded rationality: perhaps the reason why we see so many decomposable systems is that decomposable systems are the only kind that we can recognise. Adam Smith, we may recall, warned us long ago to distinguish between our models, however plausible, and the phenomena which they purport to represent; we may soothe our imaginations by attributing decomposability to systems which do not possess it. That, one might say, is the message of the ecologists; in this book I wish to apply it to the economy.

For my second observation is that even if, because of the way in which they have evolved, natural systems are indeed highly decomposable, we should not lightly assume the same properties in systems which have been deliberately crafted by man (such as multi-divisional firms). This warning is especially necessary because many man-made systems are intended to be controllable, and controllability in management is rather easily interpreted in the same way as in standard microeconomics – as requiring complete predictability of every element and individual within the system. What is not controllable is therefore liable to be excluded from the model by which the organisation is managed. But it is not thereby excluded from the behaviour of that organisation, still less from its environment.

'Interdependence is the reason why nothing comes out quite the way one wants it to' (Pfeffer and Salancik, 1978, p. 40). When it does not, our cognitive bias towards rationality is likely to attribute the result to managerial decisions (pp. 6-7); thus managers become convenient heroes or scapegoats (p. 263) – and sometimes both in quick succession, as we have surely all noticed. Human beings can handle only a limited range of interdependencies, and their boundedly rational structures are therefore likely to work well only if the significant interdependencies are few. Thus a structure which appears to be under firm control may be extremely fragile if subjected to events which have not been explicitly provided for. This is a serious potential danger in any system which is subjected to 'taut planning', as has been demonstrated by the ecological catastrophes in eastern Europe.

My third observation on Simon's theme of decomposability is that, because it relies on an evolutionary process of trial and error, at any time there may be some systems which are not decomposable, but which for some reason have not yet been subjected to a severe test. As Popper reminds us, there are always many unrefuted conjectures, and some of them will be poorly founded; Ziman (1978, p. 40), applying the same argument to his own subject, guesses that 90 per cent of the contents of the physics journals is false. We should be cautious about embracing the latest fashion, as economists, managers, investors, or just as ordinary people.

My fourth observation is that, as Simon (1969) himself points out, decomposability is not absolute. In the last resort, everything is connected to everything else. This is the insight underlying the general equilibrium method; and one of the comparative advantages of a well-educated economist should certainly be enhanced sensitivity to the pervasiveness of both substitution and complementarity. Though much better insulated against potentially disturbing messages than the system of Hahn's model, nevertheless a decomposable system, being at most almost decomposable, can preserve its equilibrium only against certain kinds and magnitudes of shock. The kind may be more important than the magnitude, but in either case its apparent stability may disappear with very little warning.

Though outside the scope of this book, I take this opportunity to mention the great value of money as a means of decomposing an extremely complex set of simultaneous decisions into a much more manageable sequence. As always, however, there are opportunity costs. Inter-temporal decomposition may lead to problems by destroying information about future consumption, and thus about the basis for present investment; but threats to the reliability of money as a store of value are far more disconcerting, and should not be evaded by convenient but implausible assumptions about perfectly-anticipated inflation.

Furthermore, 'the last resort' is often a matter of time, as Kelly points out. Effects which operate through long and indirect channels may become manifest only after lengthy intervals – years, decades, centuries, even millenia. Such effects are likely to be very hard to foresee, because they depend on the coupling of long chains of phenomena which we have learned to regard as uncoupled; and we should not expect to receive any messages which suggest the desirability of revising our theories and policies during the long period within which they appear to be working very well.

Decomposability and co-ordination

The advantages, limitations, and dangers of imposing patterns of decomposability suggest that this may be a better concept than the traditional definition of general equilibrium on which to base a theory of the co-ordination of economic activities – especially when those activities include the generation of new knowledge, and especially if we are looking for a theory of fallible co-ordination. (What better, indeed, than a theory of fallible co-ordination to link together in the imagination a tumult of jarring and discordant appearances?) Such a theoretical structure can also explain and exploit the resemblances between economists and economic agents, to which I drew attention very early in the first chapter.

'The essence of stability is not perfection but friction', suggested Winch (1971, p. 187). The kind of instant and continuous adjustment which economists often seem to imagine in an ideal competitive economy (even though it is strictly incompatible either with orthodox notions of general equilibrium or with perfect competition, which cannot exist outside equilibrium) would remove the premises for intelligent decision-making, at least by boundedly rational humans, who need at any moment some fixed points in their mental universe. There must be a framework to limit demands on their rationality, and a framework which provides a tolerable interpretation of the stream of events which they observe, including the outcomes of their previous decisions.

That is true of individuals, as Kelly has argued. If people are to work together, there is an additional requirement. Their frameworks must be compatible; they must agree what bounds to place on the interpretation of the messages from their environment, and on the responses which may be contemplated. Some constraints on choice, both one's own and other people's, are needed to make any kind of reasoned choice possible. Such agreements are often tacit – even unconscious (Arrow, 1974, p. 28), and usually ambiguous: though that ambiguity may cause problems, it also gives scope for innovation. Thus every political system has some kind of constitution, every branch of science its paradigm, every firm its structure of relationships and normal patterns of behaviour, and every market its trading practices. In each system, equilibrium may be defined as the persistence of established theories and policies – provided that we do not claim that they persist because they are correct, or optimal in any sense that can be precisely defined.

Before concentrating on economic agents, let us return briefly to the co-ordination of science, which, as Ziman (1978) insists, is a social process. Kuhn's distinction between the advances of normal science and the stable paradigm which defines what is normal, and Lakatos's distinction between the evolving protective belt and the hard-core propositions which it protects against disturbing messages, both define decomposable systems which serve to co-ordinate the generation of novelty. Specific hypotheses can be brittle, because the connecting principles can accommodate a range of actual or potential alternatives.

It is precisely because individual scientists are allowed to change their theories and policies, but only in particular ways, that the equilibrium of their scientific field is preserved. The network of inter-related hypotheses, to which Ziman (1978, pp. 39-40) draws attention, and which featured in the first chapter, is not easily disturbed by either conjectures or evidence which might threaten its co-ordination. Evolution protects equilibrium; but only if it is such evolution as the larger system can absorb. This is a fallible system, and in Kuhn's analysis it eventually but inevitably fails; hence the scientific revolutions which give the title to his most famous book. Such a system is not very well described as a general equilibrium of agents all making fully rational choices; on the other hand, the concept of general equilibrium provides an excellent means of co-ordinating the activities of a great many economists, widely dispersed, who are all seeking to generate new knowledge.

However, the structures of science are less decomposable than Kuhn and Lakatos imply. By emphasising the incorrigibility of the currently ruling paradigm, and commending as good scientific practice the highly constrained activities of normal science,

Kuhn emphasised the distinctiveness of his theme, especially in contrast to a rather popular simple caricature of Popper's falsificationist prescription, in which every component of scientific knowledge was always on the brink of rejection. In retrospect, Kuhn's argument may be regarded not as a critique of Popper, but as an extreme (and unconscious) dramatisation of Popper's sophisticated falsificationism; for Popper also emphasises the need for a framework, which includes a set of conventions, in order to avoid the Serbonian bog identified by Duhem and Quine. But in thus explaining why normal science is an efficient system for improving knowledge, Kuhn deprives himself of any means for explaining how new paradigms are formed. He makes clear how the limitations of one paradigm eventually create a need for a replacement, but by insisting that replacement must be by revolution, he abandons the prospect of analysing the contents of this revolution. That the adoption of a new paradigm is an act of faith is not in dispute; but Kuhn does not adequately consider the ways in which faith may be supported by reason. Movement between paradigms is no better handled than movement between the equilibria of economic theory, and for the same reason: the models employed are designed to explain why people do not move.

A Lakatosian research programme appears to be more flexible than a Kuhnian paradigm; yet the distinction between a paradigmatic hard core and a protective belt of normal science is maintained; and though Lakatos has more to say about the ways in which rival research programmes can be compared, he gives no more guidance on the process of their emergence. He is as concerned as Kuhn to analyse the continuity of scientific progress within a framework; but between successive or rival frameworks there is unanalysed discontinuity.

However, neither author actually succeeds in presenting a rigid framework. As is well known, the very concept of paradigm is used by Kuhn in a variety of senses (Masterman, 1970), and his case-histories exhibit neither the unanimity between adherents of a single paradigm nor the total break between rival paradigms which he appears to posit; and his admission of subparadigms to the scheme, though in some ways very helpful, effectively abolishes the sharp distinction. Nor does Lakatos provide an unequivocal means of deciding whether a particular substantial change is to be regarded as a shift between two distinct research programmes which happen to share some hardcore elements, or a progression within a single research programme in which some elements, once thought to belong in the hard core, are now correctly located in the protective belt. For an obvious and important example within economic theory, consider the status of the assumption that some markets may not clear.

There appear to be two difficulties. First, a context of discovery must be imperfectly specified if it is to produce genuine novelty, even on a small scale. Tight definitions may permit nothing more than Bayesian learning, which is not at all satisfactory as a model of science. But it may be impossible to provide the imperfections which allow a research programme to be progressive, or normal science to flourish, without simultaneously permitting some amendment to hard core propositions or reinterpretation of the paradigm. Second, all new knowledge entails some discontinuity; but even the greatest changes must be carried by some element of continuity. Normal science and scientific revolution are made of similar components, though in very different combinations. The system is not fully decomposable.

Economic co-ordination

Economic co-ordination likewise depends on networks of knowledge, which are continually being modified within the imprecise but powerful constraints of a tacitly but imperfectly agreed framework of assumptions, conventions, and procedures – what Imai (1990, p. 189) calls 'interpretation systems'. The co-ordination of dispersed and local knowledge, which Hayek has identified as the central problem of economics, may be most effectively secured within a market when that market provides the most suitable framework; but sometimes it can be better achieved within a firm, or even, possibly, by a political authority. Visible and invisible colleges each have their advantages, in the organisation of both scientific fields and the economy. It is, I suspect, because Austrian economists have not sufficiently considered the institutional requirements for co-ordination – and especially for the co-ordination of the growth of knowledge – that they have placed such overwhelming emphasis on co-ordination by market processes. Market processes can be extremely effective; but they are not always to be preferred, and often work best as one level within a decomposable structure.

Decomposability, it should be emphasised, is far from complete, as Marshall (1920) implicitly recognised by writing of each firm's internal and external organisation; Richardson (1972) explores the continuum between firm and market in some detail. Nevertheless, the organisation of an economy provides the framework within which the co-ordination problem is decomposed into sub-problems to be handled in quasi-isolation. Each part of this structure develops its own patterns of selective attention – which, let us never forget, also implies selective neglect – which allow people to work together within their shared research programme, or perhaps at higher levels of this decomposed structure, a cluster of related research programmes, without worrying about the possible interdependencies which lie beyond. The theory (or perhaps one should say set of theoretical principles) and policy which defines any such programme provides the agenda for those who work within it.

We should not interpret an agenda as a choice set, or in modern computer terminology as a menu (a comparison which I owe to Scott Moss); the list of possibilities is not closed, but open to novel conjectures. The agenda does, however, provide a focus; and some prior focus (which must be pre-rational according to the conventional definition of rationality in economics) is necessary for effective co-ordination. It is by reference to such an agenda that we can seek to explain what conjectures are proposed, what criticisms they encounter within the sub-system, what tests they are exposed to, and how messages from the sub-system's environment are interpreted and what kinds of response are considered. As with Shackle's (1972) analysis of choice, which is based on the necessary imperfection of knowledge, the accumulation of knowledge by an individual or within a group is neither random nor predetermined. It is guided towards certain kinds of discovery by the frameworks within which it is set – though the results may still be surprising. Different patterns of organisation, we must never forget, may be expected to produce different patterns of knowledge. That is why these patterns, and their differences, are so important.

If this process of learning and discovery is working well, it develops the skills and perceptions of its participants, and their confidence in the structure and practices which have proved so successful. But success has its opportunity costs. People who know how to solve their problems can get to work at once, without considering whether some other method might be more effective; they thereby become increasingly efficient, but also increasingly likely to encounter problems which are totally unexpected and which are not amenable to their efficient routines. Decomposability, we should recall, tends to degrade with time. The patterns which people impose on phenomena have necessarily a limited range of application, and the very success with which they exploit that range tends to make them increasingly careless about its limits. This danger is likely to be exacerbated by formal information systems, which are typically designed to cope with past problems, and which therefore may be worse than useless in signalling new problems. If any warning messages do arrive, they are likely to be ignored, or force-fitted into familiar categories; and if a crisis breaks, the information needed to deal with it may be impossible to obtain.

Any economic system which is to remain viable over a long period must be able to cope with unexpected change. It must be able to revise or replace policies which have worked well. Yet this ability is problematic. Two kinds of remedy may be tried, at two different system levels. One is to try to sensitize those working within a particular research programme to its limitations and to possible alternatives, thus following Menger's principle of creating private reserves against unknown but imaginable dangers, and thereby enhancing the capacity for internal adaptation. This is the way in which Shell try to use scenarios. But reserves have costs; and it may be better, from a system-wide perspective, to accept the vulnerability of a sub-system in order to exploit its efficiency, while relying on the reserves which are the natural product of a variety of sub-systems. This is not, of course, a strategy which would appeal to anyone who, like Kelly, is primarily concerned with the welfare of the individual.

Research programmes, we should recall, are imperfectly specified, and two groups starting with the same research programme (if indeed we can define what that means) are likely to become progressively differentiated by their experience, if there are no strong pressures to keep them closely aligned. The long-run equilibrium of the larger system might therefore by preserved by substitution between sub-systems as circumstances change. External selection may achieve the same overall purpose as internal adaptation – but only if the system has generated adequate variety from which the selection may be made. An obvious corollary, which has been emphasised by Klein (1977) is that attempts to preserve sub-system stability may wreck the larger system. That should not be a threatening notion to economists; it also happens to be exemplified by Marshall's conception of the long-period equilibrium of the industry as a population equilibrium, which is sustained by continued change in the membership of that population. The tendency to variation is not only a chief cause of progress; it is also an aid to stability in a changing environment (Eliasson, 1991). The homogeneity which is conducive to the attainment of conventional welfare optima is a threat to the resilience which an economy needs.

Schumpeter (1934), of course, goes well beyond Marshall. Whole industries become habituated to rules of behaviour which have been tested by experience, and thus embody the logic of static efficiency; but they are incapable of escaping from their routines and are therefore destroyed by innovation. Schumpeter's system is strictly decomposed into routine-followers and innovators, and this entails a substantial adjustment cost, while its members struggle towards a new equilibrium, with no guidance from Schumpeter or, apparently, anywhere else.

At some level, an economy – and indeed any community – needs to conserve the ability to adapt to new circumstances (Klein, 1977, p. 147). Economists may reasonably leave to psychologists the investigation of personal resilience – though being ready to consider the implications of such investigations for consumer theory and agency problems, to take two obvious examples; but they should place on their own professional agenda the problem of resilience in firms and markets. On the level of self-interest, the exercise of modifying the research programmes of economics in this way should help to conserve the ability of the economics profession to adapt to new problems – which happen, of course, to be very old. In the following three chapters, I shall try to suggest how this might be done.

4
Firms

In this chapter we shall consider a firm as a device for the co-ordination and use of particular kinds of knowledge, including the co-ordination of knowledge generation, by the imposition of an interpretative framework on a problem area which is treated as if it were separable from other problem areas. We are thereby imposing a framework on our own analysis which does not naturally suggest an emphasis on production functions or agency problems. It suggests something much more Marshallian.

The growth of the firm

As I have recently attempted to present Marshall's conception of the firm as one of the forms of organisation which aid knowledge (Whitaker, 1990, pp. 108-26), I will turn instead to Edith Penrose's *Theory of the Growth of the Firm* (1959), which is in most respects thoroughly Marshallian – despite having only two references to Marshall, who is then wrongly identified in the index. The growth of the firm is not to be explained, in her theory, by the allocation of resources to an optimal growth path, which is more or less what we get when Marris (1964) tries to represent her ideas in a formal model of growth equilibrium. (Marris's discussion, much of which escapes his model, is closer to Penrose, and indeed develops parts of her analysis in illuminating ways.) Growth depends on the creation of an organisation which structures the growth of knowledge; and the rate and direction of growth are both heavily influenced by that organisation. A firm is 'a pool of resources the utilisation of which is organised in an administrative framework' (Penrose, 1959, p. 149); and it is 'the

heterogeneity ... of the productive services available or poten-
tially available from its resources that gives each firm its unique
character' (p. 75). Each firm creates its own capabilities from its
particular socially-organised set of skills, which are partly inar-
ticulate and continually changing. Demsetz (1988, p. 150) has of-
fered a similar conception of a firm as 'a bundle of commitments
to technology, personnel, and methods, all contained and con-
strained by an insulating layer of information that is specific to
the firm'.

What the firm knows how to do, in Mrs Penrose's presenta-
tion, is what its managers know how to do, or how to get done;
and that depends on the pattern of experience, and therefore
changes over time in ways which cannot be foreseen in any de-
tail. She does not pay much attention to the development of skill
and knowledge at the technological level, though she clearly
does not think that firms have common access to production
functions. Nor does she consider the need to interpret experience
– the messages which her managers receive from their environ-
ment are unambiguous, and apparently lead directly to new the-
ories and policies, though these are not assumed to be optimal.
She explicitly confines her analysis to firms which succeed in
growing, believing that no theory of growth can explain mistakes
(p. 41). As should be plain, I take the contrary view, that a theory
of co-ordination should be capable of explaining both success
and failure.

On the other hand, Mrs Penrose not only recognises but builds
on two other important features. First, each firm's evolution will
tend to differentiate its knowledge and capabilities from those of
other firms; within a diversified firm, this process will be at work
in each business unit. Kelly (1963, p. 75) insists that learning 'is
not something that happens to a person on occasion; it is what
makes him a person in the first place'. We simply need to replace
'person' by 'firm' or 'business unit' to suggest how each such
unit acquires its unique character as an interpretative system,
construing events and acting on the basis of its interpretations –
though we must be wary of treating a business unit as if it were a
single individual.

Much knowledge comes from personal experience, especially
knowledge about what can be achieved within a particular work-
ing relationship, and this is a product of time and circumstance

(Penrose, 1959, p. 46), much of it not easily communicated to outsiders (pp. 53-4). Thus simply bringing in more people is not enough to ensure successful growth. Time must be allowed for their integration into an effective group (pp. 46-8). Firm-specific evolution is important – a theme which we may nowadays associate particularly with the work of Keith Pavitt at the University of Sussex. Pavitt (1987, p. 124) is inclined to argue that firm-specific expertise is not easy to transfer because accumulated incremental change may be difficult to distinguish in retrospect from radical change (as I suggested earlier) – especially from the viewpoint of a potential adopter; Mrs Penrose is content to assume that firms tend not to try.

The other important feature is the administrative framework, which enters into her theory in two ways. In the terms which I have been using, it provides an equilibrium structure of theory and policy within which individual knowledge can evolve without threatening organisational coherence; but that equilibrium itself is the consequence of an evolutionary process during which managers learn to operate effectively together within a particular environment. It is this evolutionary process which generates the growth of managerial services – or reduction in governance costs – which is so important to her analysis, and also shapes the content and scope of those services.

'The possibilities of using services change with changes in knowledge' (Penrose, 1959, p. 76); but 'no firm ever perceives the complete range of services available from any resource, because the range of services recognised is for the most part confined by the management's existing ideas as to possible combinations' (p. 86). What combinations of the services which are recognised (or imagined, for we should not ignore the possibility that there are imaginary services included in managerial analyses of strengths and weaknesses) will be put to use depends on the managerial perception of markets. The perceived scope for using the firm's own particular collection of services defines that firm's productive opportunity (p. 31). This is clearly a subjective concept, which is likely to be incomplete, and in some respects false. It should not be confused with more recent formulations of strategic choice as a rational response to a correctly identified environment by a firm which is treated as a corporate individual (Melin, 1987, pp. 157-9).

Mrs Penrose recognises the possibility of error in these subjective estimates, but discusses neither the circumstances which are most conducive to error nor the possible consequences; she does, however, emphasise that behaviour depends not on the objective environment, which 'is not discoverable before the event' (p. 41) but on the expectations of the firm's decision-makers. The consequences of that behaviour will of course depend on the objective environment; but that environment is partly created by the actions of other firms, which are influenced by their own subjective expectations. Because of her focus on the individual firm, Mrs Penrose does not pursue this issue; it will receive some attention in the next chapter.

She discusses instead the relationship between managerial and entrepreneurial skills, which she relates in Schumpeterian fashion to a distinction between the execution of ideas and their conception. But whereas Schumpeter sees management as locked into routines, for Mrs Penrose the execution of ideas generates fresh knowledge, and so 'the productive opportunity of a firm will change even in the absence of any change in external circumstances or in fundamental technological knowledge' (p. 56). Messages from the environment lead to modification or extensions of theory and policy; thus the potential for innovation grows out of the firm's routine operations, just as Marshall's businessman finds the basis for his experiments in the results of his daily business. But the use made of this knowledge depends, in Mrs Penrose's view, on the willingness to commit resources to uncertain prospects; it is determined by preferences rather than ideas, which apparently will come to those who are prepared to look (pp. 33-4). That is not to deny that managers will vary in their entrepreneurial skills as well as their entrepreneurial inclinations, nor indeed that entrepreneurial as well as managerial services are partly a product of the firm's own history (p. 35).

Mrs Penrose's analysis of the direction of a firm's expansion is worth some notice. The managerial costs of growth, and therefore the managerial impediments to growth, she argues, are likely to be lowest in familiar activities – but only if this growth does not involve a struggle for market share or productive resources with powerful rivals (p. 209). The likelihood of such a struggle may be related to the stage of the product-market life-cycle, and the managerial impediments, as Marshall emphasised, to the life-

cycle of the firm itself. In such circumstances, growth through ac-
quisition may involve lower costs, because managerial services
have already been developed in the acquired business. However
the integration of two interpretative systems may give rise to
problems which she does not specifically mention (p. 128), but
which are inherent in that process of gradual differentiation of
knowledge and procedures between firms – even in the same in-
dustry – which is at the core of her theory.

Either the apparent limitation of prospects in the firm's exist-
ing market (p. 105) or the development of capabilities (whether
technological or marketing) which seem to have attractive uses
elsewhere (pp. 115-16) may suggest that the most productive op-
portunities lie in diversification. What matters, of course, is the
firm's perceived comparative advantage, not only in relation to
firms already in the market which is targeted, but also in relation
to other potential entrants; formidable entry barriers from which
one firm is exempt may serve as a strong inducement to that par-
ticular firm, as Richardson (1960, 1990, pp. 62-8) has pointed out.

Perhaps because of her concern to explain how firms succeed
in growing, Mrs Penrose does not draw attention to the ease with
which diversification options may be misjudged. Members of a
firm may have learnt so well what is important, what simplifica-
tions work, and what can be safely assumed about the behaviour
of other people – colleagues, customers, and competitors – in the
kinds of business to which they have become accustomed, that
they no longer have a framework – especially a structure of con-
tacts and communication – which would allow them to cope ef-
fectively with a new period of learning, or even to recognise any
need for it. People who share a common tradition may operate a
highly decomposed system very efficiently on the basis of tacit
knowledge; but such a system is likely to be capable of only cer-
tain limited kinds of change. What is worse, these limits may be
almost impossible to discover except by collision. Earl (1984, pp.
112-19) surveys some of these collisions.

On the other hand, Mrs Penrose does discuss a danger which
has become much more widely acknowledged in recent years:
the tendency for a diversified firm to require increasing commit-
ments in very different lines of business in order to maintain a
viable position in each (pp. 131-6), commitments which the com-
pany strategists may be unable or unwilling to provide. Many

companies have given this as the reason for reductions in their range, thus tacitly admitting the inadequacy of their past theories and policies. Companies such as BTR and Hanson, by comparison, claim to restrict their activities to mature business which use simple or fully-developed technologies; these should make modest demands on managerial services, and operate successfully on the basis of proven theories and policies in a highly decomposed structure which is controlled by financial, not strategic management. This can be a very successful formula for companies which correctly identify the businesses which fit it; it can be disastrous if they go wrong. (For a detailed investigation, see Goold and Campbell, 1987.)

Routines

Nelson and Winter's (1982) analysis of organisational skills and routines, though formulated in different terms and taking its inspiration from Schumpeter, may readily be interpreted as a development of the Marshallian ideas in Mrs Penrose's theory. Nelson and Winter clearly approve of Marshall, but they are so attracted by Schumpeter's bold design that they do not recognise how Marshallian is their conception of the firm, notably in the differences between firms in their skills and perceptions. Their analysis may also be translated – with the inevitable losses associated with all translation – into the language of evolving theories and policies within an equilibrium framework.

Like Marris, Nelson and Winter have more to say than they know how to incorporate in their formal models, and the evolution of a firm's routines, by a process which Kelly would have fitted comfortably into his own analytical scheme, is probably the most important element to be excluded from the Markov processes which they simulate. Knowledge, they recognise, is not completely expressible, and therefore cannot be precisely specified; its scope is uncertain, and the experience which provides evidence for its reliability cannot be fully recovered. As Ziman (1978) also recognises, we accept many propositions because we believe, without specific enquiry, that they have been rigorously tested by someone else; and our belief is not always justified. Occasionally it produces a scientific scandal; in everyday life it is an accepted hazard.

By a process of trial and error, which may be carefully designed or extremely casual – a non-random sample of one is not uncommon – people establish patterns of interpretation and action, which Nelson and Winter call routines. By choosing, like Kelly, to treat people as scientists, we can attribute these routines of interpretation and action to theories and policies, noting that theories, as Simon (1982, 2, p. 142) points out, allow us to economise on facts, and that policies, according to Heiner (1983), drastically simplify the making of decisions. An established set of theories and policies, including those which link together activities which need to be mutually consistent, constitute an equilibrium, and provide the elements of rigidity which help to preserve it.

This equilibrium includes routines for making product, for collecting information, for search (in laboratory, market, or manager's office), for operating decisions, and for strategic review. Associated with each routine is a cue, or set of cues, which call it into use: these may include the arrival of a partly-finished product at a work-station, a telephone call from a customer, an unfavourable variance underlined in a monthly report, a government announcement – and many others. As these examples suggest, many routines act as cues to subsequent routines. Some of these routines and cues may be deliberately created, but in time will probably diverge substantially from the original intentions; others may evolve from a sequence of narrowly-focused decisions.

Cues may be represented as messages from the environment, often immediate, sometimes more remote, which are construed in terms of the prevailing theory, and elicit a response which is guided by current policy. This representation, it should be recognised, imposes too much rationality on what is normally a simple pattern of stimulus and response; but it does allow the equilibrium to encompass incremental change, of which Nelson and Winter identify three kinds.

The first is a continuation of the process of trial and error, focused, as Adam Smith pointed out, by the particular pattern of specialisation employed, in which routines (or theories and policies) are gradually modified by the interpretation of events, whether these result from conscious decision, accidental variation, or outside influences. Nelson and Winter's analysis of this process should be supplemented by a reminder that firms do not learn simply by doing, but by interpreting the apparent consequences of what they have done; and this interpretation depends upon a background of beliefs which may be rather poorly defined. Nor should we forget that the process results not only in the enhancement of skills which are practised but also in the decay of those which cease to be used. We learn to forget about what is no longer relevant. That may matter very little, if progress is linear; but sometimes it is not.

Productive improvements, especially in science-based industries, may follow some kind of natural trajectory, guided by a research programme, as has been suggested by Dosi (1982). However, such a trajectory may be apparent only by hindsight, and it should never be lightly assumed to be the only possible trajectory. This cumulative process may yield the organisation a cumulative advantage; but the consequent corroboration of the routines for achieving improvement may be transformed into a serious disadvantage if the line of progress shifts to a different trajectory. This is not an unfamiliar story, and has been made the basis of a new recipe for business success (Foster, 1986).

The second kind of change results from changes in personnel, which, despite the best efforts of training programmes, usually bring a slightly different perspective (as Kelly's definition of personality implies and as Arrow (1974, p. 59) recognises) and possibly some difference in motivation. The third is produced by routines which are designed for that purpose: procedures for investigating markets, production methods, possible new products, or even organisation structures. Such procedures may be guided by explicit strategies, corporate vision, tradition, or opportunism. Each firm changes in its own way and in its own direction; the resultant variety is exposed to selection in the environment on which they all depend for a continued flow of resources.

Organisational coherence

Large organisations are divided into sub-systems; and the principle of decomposability applies here too. The co-ordination of activities between sub-systems is separated out from co-ordination within each sub-system and handled by linking routines, which may be deliberately created (for example by the establishment of reporting systems) or the product of incremental change. But because decomposability is never complete, organisational design remains problematic, as Earl (1984, pp. 162-72), demonstrates. Organisational boundaries allow, and usually encourage, the development of different theories and policies which appear to fit local circumstances, and are a major factor in determining what potential interdependencies are ignored in the evolution and refinement of these theories and policies. They limit as well as protect; they have the virtues of their defects, but also the defects of their virtues.

The survival of a business depends on its ability to elicit the contributions which it needs in order to remain in business – from, among others, its customers, suppliers, workers, managers, bankers, and governmental agencies. At any one time, some of these contributors will be more difficult to satisfy than others, and there is likely to be particular attention to the routines which are intended to meet, bypass, or counterweight their demands. But the balance of pressures may change, and this may call into question current theories and policies. In particular, the current theory of decomposability is likely to break down. Increasing consciousness of the defects of an existing structure may therefore lead to restructuring, as we often see; and the relationships between the firm and its environment may evolve in ways which change the balance of advantage between alternative structures.

Chandler's (1962) account of the emergence of the product division structure is just the most striking example of a very common switch between schemes of decomposition – or equilibrium frameworks for evolution. The subsequent extension of Chandler's analysis into the proposition that diversified firms should adopt M-form structures has tended to obscure the difficulty of choosing between alternative versions of that form. (Williamson, for example, has paid little attention to it.) A significant reordering of priorities implies substantial changes of theory and policy, which are rarely achieved easily. It is also likely to entail changes in status, and may be resisted for that reason: insistence on preserving the higher status of the heavy electrical departments in British electrical engineering companies has been blamed for the failure of these companies to cater adequately for the rapidly developing demand for domestic electrical appliances in the 1950s (Rogers, 1963) – thus providing an entrepreneurial opportunity for John Bloom, whose novel theories and policies produced spectacular success, followed by equally spectacular disaster. It is not therefore surprising that successful restructuring is usually associated with extensive changes among senior management.

Nelson and Winter do not present their ideas in this way; instead they draw attention to the importance of linking routines and, in the tradition of Cyert and March (1963), to the ways in which sub-unit independence is protected by ambiguity and the avoidance of dangerous issues. Since Arrow's impossibility theorem applies to organisations, they must operate by coalition rather than consensus; some conflicts must therefore be hidden. The very fact that contracts within a firm must be imperfectly specified if people are to have freedom to improve their theories and policies helps to create room for such practices.

Organisational truces help to maintain system equilibrium while permitting change at sub-system levels. They are buttressed by such factors as local rationality, sequential attention to goals, and the use of budgetary procedures to define protected space – if you keep within your budget, no one has the right to interfere, so try to make sure you have a budget that you can keep within. A second-best solution is to control the information which is compared with the budget. By one route or another, all control systems must be expected to generate misinformation. But as Nelson and Winter point out, the desire to preserve an equilibrium is an obstacle to changes which affect more than one sub-system. Since the terms of the truce, like so much else within an organisation, are not explicitly agreed, all parties are likely to be sensitive to possible breaches, and this will constrain responses to messages which appear to suggest a deficiency in current theory or policy.

Thus a proposed change which is in itself perfectly acceptable to one group may be opposed by them for fear of giving the impression that they would tolerate other changes which would be much less welcome; and if the originators of a possible change put a high value on preserving the coalition – or if they merely prefer a quiet life – they may forbear proposing it. The organisational psychologist Chris Argyris (1985) has drawn attention to the number of issues which are undiscussable within an organisation, and the ways in which the undiscussability of issues itself can become undiscussable. This phenomenon is not unknown in less formal organisations, including families and groups of friends – not to mention academic disciplines.

Any equilibrium so buttressed will be extremely resistant to messages from the environment, to the extent, very often, of closing down channels of communication. Such a rigid system, in which little decomposability remains, is likely to be very susceptible to collapse; but even a general recognition of its vulnerability may not be sufficient to induce reform: indeed the urgent desire to preserve stability, against the odds, may be strongest in an organisation whose members fear that it is not resilient (to borrow an argument from my former colleague Mick Common). These are the circumstances in which undiscussability shrouds the most crucial issues. The German Democratic Republic provides an extreme example. People are not likely to relinquish theories and policies, however obviously flawed, unless they can see some prospect of an acceptable alternative. That, of course, is why I am trying to persuade readers of this book that there is another way of doing economics than that proclaimed by Gary Becker.

The need to preserve a coalition of interests is one reason why it is sometimes more important to have agreement on the facts than to get the facts right, as Simon observed. But even if there were no differences of interest, it may still be more important to have agreement on the kinds of theories and policies to be considered than to have the best kind. Both visible and invisible colleges are unlikely to be very efficient without a framework – which, of course, is not to say that any framework will do. From our understanding of the fundamental problems of knowledge we can be pretty certain that any framework that we use will be incomplete, and probably in some respects positively unhelpful; and that will be true of the frameworks used within a business. (Just think, for example, of management accounts, with their allocations of common costs, or of the misrepresentations of reality which are portrayed by organisation charts.) Some misrepresentations are inevitable; the behaviour of an organisation, and the knowledge which it generates, will be influenced by what misrepresentations they are. The impact of a message from the economy depends on what theory or policy it is compared with.

A remarkably similar analysis of organisational coherence

may be found in Arrow's *Limits of Organization* (1974), which uses neoclassical methods to subvert comprehensively (though apparently not by design) the neoclassical concept of the optimising firm. Organisations make costly and irreversible commitments to information systems (p. 39) and the coding systems which they employ (p. 55). The particular form taken by each results from the accidents of history (pp. 41, 56), and the product of this historical pattern gives each firm its distinct identity (p. 55) – just as Mrs Penrose had said – and, by a slight extension of Arrow's argument about the direction of learning (pp. 41-2), conditions its distinctive productive opportunity.

Arrow also points to the penalties of efficiency (p. 49): an information system (and, by extension, a theory and policy) precisely tailored to current expectations is likely to inhibit adaptation to a changed environment (p. 54). In Menger's terms, the organisation is fully committed in what is now the wrong direction, and has no reserves. The problem may well be even worse, since the system will filter out information which does not match expectations (p. 75), and action may be impossible without a crisis (p. 52). As Arrow observes, commitment to past purposes is a familiar basis for tragedy (p. 29). Arrow does not explore the implications of his argument for the practices of economists.

Demsetz (1988, p. 155) also points out that members of an organisation may maintain commitments to each other and to the routines which link them long past the time when external circumstances call for change. But although he recognises the motivation to preserve human capital, he does not explore the concept of human capital in Marshallian terms, as complex structures of knowledge, or, in Hahn's terminology, as clusters of theories and policies. Still less does he recognise the inhibitions against the abandonment of an interpretative framework which has long seemed to make sense of an organisation's work, and of personal contributions to that work.

Organisational pathology

To conclude this chapter, I would like to draw attention to a problem within organisations which is equivalent to that briefly discussed at the end of the first chapter. Frameworks, theories, and policies, in business as in economics and everyday life, all belong in Popper's World 3; and the life of World 3 can generate its own issues, which may not map at all readily on to the underlying phenomena. Issues and decisions may simply be artefacts of the internal system.

Let me offer a few examples. One of the commonest is the displacement of objectives. Too often, the purpose of planning is to produce an acceptable document (as my university colleagues would readily agree), and organisations are rearranged so that they can be represented tidily on paper. The first response to any request to cut costs is very often to have them reallocated to another part of the business. Universities are very good at this too; indeed early retirement schemes have been widely used to allow a particular university to obtain the services of faculty most of whose income is no longer chargeable to that university.

People look for simplifications and pursue them relentlessly. Some years ago a management consultant remarked to me that managers were continually looking for a 'golden key' to unlock all their problems. In management writing and in management practice we have seen a succession of these keys: one that is currently fashionable is Total Quality Management. They are not unknown in economics. Almost invariably they are used where they don't fit, as well as where they do; they usually result in game-playing; and even when taken seriously, are likely to become progressively detached from the company's environment. When small cars began to take a significant share of the American market, a General Motors executive announced that GM would not make small cars because 'you squeeze out value faster than you squeeze out cost'. How many people pressured into a Total Quality programme would recognise the fallacy in that argument? How would they react to the current example of Ecover, whose environmentally-friendly products cost more and do not perform as well as their orthodox competitors, but have been gaining market share?

The chief scientist of the team which became the Airborne Early Warning Division of Marconi Avionics, awarded a crucial and very expensive British defence contract, explained in a letter to *The Times* how that Division's work came to be confined, in the language of this book, to the problems which were defined by its own theories. The team had completed a ground model of a simpler airborne early warning system before that project was cancelled in 1970; thereafter, although the team generated studies and proposals for complete systems,

no radar which was not trivial in comparison with the AEW was actually made and operated to give experience in the advanced and advancing techniques which we were so confidently designing on paper ... the very lack of continuing development on a significant scale which made the undertaking one of risk masked from us the full extent of the risks we were taking. (Whitehead, 1987)

Any further messages from the environment, it appears, were assumed to be unnecessary; the team was confident that it was using the correct theory. It is not surprising that the contract ended in costly and embarrassing failure.

It may be some consolation to know that the British are not uniquely capable of such débâcles. Indeed, the Americans, once again, have managed to produce something much bigger and better. For a case-study of a company spending hundreds of millions of dollars in pursuit of internally-generated objectives by internally-generated means, I commend Margaret Graham's account of RCA and the video disc, entitled *The Business of Research* (1986).

The project was defined to fit RCA's theory of the market, which reflected its experience as a leading producer of radios, television sets, and records, and its association with one of the three US broadcasting networks, NBC. This theory postulated a mass-market for technically-advanced pre-packaged entertainment; the logical next major development after colour television was therefore ready-made visual programmes, and the equipment for consumers to show them: an entertainment system. This theory of the next step was encapsulated in the company brandname: Selectavision. The company failed to heed Drucker's (1964, p. 87) warning that 'the customer rarely buys what the business thinks it sells'. That consumers might wish to make their own entertainment, even in the trivial sense of recording television programmes for watching later, seems to have occurred to no one in RCA. No one doubted the theory or the policy; past corroboration was assumed to exclude any possibility of future falsification.

The organisation did possess enough decomposability to allow people to initiate work on several different technologies in different parts of the business, and this enabled some options to be preserved for a time; but the video disc technology emerged triumphant. It emerged triumphant because RCA had acquired a reputation for technological leadership, notably in the development of colour television, which many people wanted to preserve and enhance. They had a theory of company excellence, and a policy which depended on it. Members of the Research Department placed their own special emphasis on this objective, which would ensure the status of their department as the prime mover of company strategy (a very common kind of displacement of objectives). Video disc offered just the right technical challenge for both general and sectional objectives; tape recording, by contrast, was dismissed as a 'spent technology'. RCA's theory of competition featured Philips and Grundig, with CBS as a possible entrant; Japanese companies were considered to be potential contributors of royalty income.

The one exception to this internally-defined problem set was provided by a senior appointment from Ford, which was apparently based on the theory that Ford knew how to drive projects to completion. The man appointed duly applied his Ford-based theories and policies, which assumed that all projects used only fully-proven technology, and pushed researchers into providing plans which complied with the target dates imposed, but not with the requirements of the project. The collision between RCA and Ford models of theory and policy generated too many threatening messages within the company to allow anyone time to think about messages from the economy. But in the end, the economy delivered some messages which could not be ignored. It first selected out the video disc, which lost $580 million in the three years after its introduction, and then the whole collection of theories and policies which produced it, by ending the separate existence of RCA.

5
Markets

In this chapter, we shift our attention to the level of the market system, which Nelson and Winter (1982, p. 277) characterise as '(in part) a device for conducting and evaluating experiments in economic behaviour and organisation'. Plans are tested in the market, and so is the organisation which produced them. That is not the standard conception, though it is not far from Marshall's; and I have to say that economists have no theory of how markets work. A theory of market equilibrium is not a theory of how markets work, as Frank Hahn, for example, has often pointed out. Even the Austrians, who make much use of the phrase 'market process', have little to say about the way such processes operate. All I can offer here is some suggestions towards a theory, derived from the connecting principles which I have been using in this book.

Market relationships

Let us return to Adam Smith. The potential gains from the division of labour extend far beyond what can be achieved by co-operation between colleagues; to achieve these gains requires the co-operation of people who do not know each other well, and of people who do not know each other at all. Such co-operation, Smith argues, can be achieved in a system of free markets which make effective use of self-interest. But we should note how self-interest is to be used: what matters is not that all people should seek their own advantages, but that they should offer advantages to those with whom they deal (Smith, 1976b, p. 27).

This is the essence of the marketing point of view. The customers of a chemical company do not buy chemicals, or even chemical effects; they buy solutions to problems. What the chemical company needs to know, therefore, is a set of answers to the following questions. What are the customer's problems? How much is a solution worth – or in contemporary jargon, what is its added value? Which of these problems can be solved by using the distinctive skills and resources which are available to the company? What alternative solutions might be available or in prospect through the use of other distinctive skills and resources – which might embody totally unrelated technologies – available in other organisations, and how effective and expensive are they likely to be? What, in a phrase, in the company's productive opportunity? In developing these questions we have extended Smith's formulation to include Menger's emphasis on the growth of knowledge, and also Kirzner's (1973) emphasis on the importance of allowing people to profit from private knowledge by making it available to others, typically in the form of goods or services.

As an aid to understanding customers' problems, we should not underrate the importance of sympathy, in its eighteenth century sense, which is perhaps now better rendered by 'empathy'. The ability to sense what customers will buy, or, more generally, what are the potential benefits of any deal or alliance from the point of view of the other party, is indeed highly regarded. But it needs to be supplemented by developing channels of information, and that is a very important function of a market. The value of price signals is now well recognised, but a market in which specialisation is matched by integration, according to Marshall's general rule, can offer much more. It provides a framework within which we can supplement our direct knowledge of how to do things with indirect knowledge of how to get them done. 'The function of competition is here precisely to teach us *who* will serve us well: which grocer or travel agency, which department store or hotel, which doctor or solicitor, we can expect to provide the most satisfactory solution for whatever particular personal problem we may have to face' (Hayek, 1946, p. 97). Notice that expectations are directed, not towards a fixed list of goods, but towards the supplier's capabilities, or what we might choose to call the supplier's routines or research programme.

Hayek emphasises the advantage to consumers, not only of

being able to choose between suppliers, but also of developing continuing relationships with them in order to acquire, use, and test knowledge. But there are advantages to suppliers too. Peter Drucker (1964, p. 85) had good reason to declare that 'the purpose of business is to create a customer'. The benefits of regular custom are not to be found primarily – and perhaps not at all – in the profit opportunities of a monopolistic demand curve, but, first, in lower transactions costs, second, in the information content of regular purchases, and third, in the communication channels which are created. Nor should we forget that many suppliers do not deal with the final consumers whose problems they are helping to solve; unless they take the trouble to communicate directly with those consumers, they are dependent on intermediaries for knowledge which may be crucial to their continued prosperity. Whether these intermediaries are a source of reliable knowledge – or indeed of any knowledge beyond that of price and quantity – depends on the relationships which are created with them.

Austrian economists have rightly drawn attention to the virtues of a market system in promoting the effective use of dispersed and incomplete knowledge; but they have had little more to say than other economists about the ways in which markets can structure the generation of knowledge. To suggest how this process may be analysed I shall draw on the similarities between a market and a scientific community, which I noted in Chapter 2.

The market as framework

Nelson and Winter's formulation, quoted at the beginning of this chapter, should remind us that the evaluation of experiments is not straightforward. The Duhem-Quine problem applies to markets; and the market test cannot therefore be a test of truth in any simple sense. If a market is to operate as a consistent selection device, and to provide a framework within which experiments can be conducted, its participants need a fair measure of agreement on the theories and policies which they apply. Economists often evade this difficulty by assuming that every experiment consists simply of choosing a quantity, and is judged by the profit which ensues.

The agreement between market participants may be tacit, but

it need not be. Indeed, the market may work better if its messages are not simply of acceptance or rejection, but include specific criticisms and suggestions. This is particularly important when organisations are generating and offering collections of characteristics, or what is sometimes called 'a total marketing package'. Without some helpful voices, as well as exit, it may not be easy for a firm to interpret the messages which it receives from the economy in response to such complex conjectures. As in all other contexts, it is only by assuming the truth of many hypotheses, any of which may be false, that we can bring a single hypothesis to a severe – though still fallible – test. In his discussion of entrepreneurship, where this difficulty is most acute, Mark Casson (1982) points to the advantage of refusing to change price, whatever the messages received, in order to try to isolate the effect of other parts of the package, and thus to judge more effectively the need to revise the theory which underlies the policy.

For a well-established business, an important part of the evolutionary process described by Edith Penrose (1959) is the creation and testing of reliable theories about market response – what might be called, according to preference or convenience, the market's research programme, market institutions, or market routines. Nelson and Winter's analysis of routines and their evolution appears readily applicable to well-developed markets, in which certain ways of doing business come to be accepted. There are various methods of determining prices – for example, they may be set by buyers, sellers, or intermediaries, settled by bargaining, or arrived at by one of several auctioning procedures – but there is rarely more than one method in use in one market. In addition, the customs of the trade usually prescribe such matters as credit terms, after-sales service, and conformity to market standards, including compatibility with other suppliers' products. These constitute the policy of the market, and both facilitate and constrain the decisions of those who participate in it.

If the firm can identify the principal features of market equilibrium, it can thereby gauge the amount and kind of discretion which it may use in generating and using new products and new services. (It is, of course, not possible to discover precisely what as-yet-uninvented novelty will be acceptable.) A firm may do this more quickly, and more surely, if it seeks to establish channels of communication. I have already drawn attention (in Chapter 2) to Marshall's little-noticed discussion of the need for a businessman to develop his 'external organisation' – and his emphasis, being Marshall, on the time which it necessarily takes to do so. The businessman's interest in finding out what is going on, what his customers think, what his competitors are doing, and what new opportunities seem to be emerging, is a natural complement to his interest in developing new products and new processes. Plans must finally be tested in the market, to use Kirzner's (1973, p. 10) phrase; but it can save time, expense, and disappointment if they can be tried out beforehand – even though such trials, like all test procedures, may be misleading.

Like the evaluation of hypotheses by communities of scholars, the market test is interpersonal rather than impersonal, and intersubjective rather than objective; it is moreover a test of compatibility with the current institutions of the market. If the market rejects a conjecture, it may be the market which is wrong. Indeed, the Schumpeterian concept of innovation implies that, in relation to the entrepreneur's conjecture, the market is indeed wrong, and must be bypassed or reconstructed in order to validate the new combination which is incompatible with established routines. Markets operate on shared assumptions about knowledge, but no matter how many people share an assumption, it may still be false – or, perhaps more often in economic affairs, have become inadequate in new circumstances. We shall have a little more to say about the relationship between market routines and innovation in the next chapter.

Markets and hierarchies

Meanwhile, let us see what we can deduce from our exploration of the problems of co-ordinating the growth of knowledge about the relationship between markets and hierarchies. In a highly decomposable economy, each market would comprise a group of hierarchies; that is the simplified pattern of Nelson and Winter's analysis, which allows them to study in detail how a hierarchy works – and incidentally how much can be achieved without using formal relationships to transmit either information or instructions. On the other hand, the development of economic analysis has raised the question, first systematically explored by

Coase (1937), why there should be any need for hierarchies in order to achieve efficient co-ordination. Market failure, it was (too easily) accepted, could provide a case for the activities of government; no case whatever had been made for the activities of business firms, in which people worked to orders rather than to prices.

Coase's explanation depended on the costs of organising transactions among an anonymous multitude and in response to changing data – in effect the still-unresolved problem of finding an equilibrium even if its formal existence could be established. After a generation in which, as Coase (1972, p. 63) noted, his article was 'much cited but little used', it has produced a substantial literature, which has been dominated by Oliver Williamson (1985, 1986). Coase, very reasonably, had pointed out that setting up pure market transactions might be very costly even if all market participants were, in effect, motivated solely by a zeal for co-operation in finding Pareto-optimal bargains; Williamson, equally reasonably, pointed out that self-interest might imply other motives, which could entail much higher costs, especially when these motives interacted with bounded rationality.

After his earlier work on managerial objectives (1964) and the problems of management control (1967), Williamson subsequently adopted a highly-simplified view both of organisational decision-making and of the operation of markets. This has enabled him to generate a few powerful hypotheses about the relative advantages of market exchange and internal organisation (especially in respect of vertical integration) and the properties of alternative organisational structures, in particular the advantages of product divisions in securing managerial discipline through internal financial markets. These hypotheses have been produced, and their appeal enhanced, by the derivation of something very like rational choice equilibria: the most efficient form is chosen by agents who correctly predict the consequences of the alternatives.

Since the theme of this book is that something other than rational choice equilibria are needed for an adequate understanding of the co-ordination of the growth of knowledge, it is not surprising that Williamson's analytical framework is not quite sufficient for our purposes, nor that its limitations are to be found precisely in its avoidance of the problem of knowledge.

These limitations affect Williamson's treatment of both markets and hierarchies.

One aspect of a firm's external organisation which deserves special attention is its relationship with other firms whose activities are closely complementary. The relationship between Marks and Spencer and its suppliers, or between car manufacturers and the suppliers of major components, provide obvious examples. Such relationships may give rise to the phenomena identified by Williamson, such as the opportunity to exploit a partner's highly-specialised assets, which threaten to stultify beneficial collaboration; they may therefore, as Williamson suggests, have to be brought under a single ownership if such collaboration is to be possible.

However, as G. B. Richardson (1972) pointed out before Williamson developed his theory, this does not always happen. Richardson draws attention to the frequency of close working relationships between independent companies, centred on goods or services which are carefully tailored to the customer's requirements – precisely the situation which Williamson assumes must provide such inducements to opportunism as to prove unworkable, and which must therefore give way to vertical integration. But Richardson argues that in many such situations it is vertical integration which is likely to prove unworkable, because activities which are closely complementary may nevertheless be highly dissimilar, and therefore difficult to manage effectively within a single structure.

Williamson ignores Marshall's emphasis on the importance of a thorough knowledge of one's trade, and Mrs Penrose's insistence on the relevance of slowly-developed skills to particular contexts – even though in the absence of such factors it would appear that the scope for opportunism would not be very great. His firms are little more than a portfolio of production functions under expert financial management. But Richardson (1972, p. 888) points out that conventional production functions abstract from knowledge and skill, whereas the organisation of industry is guided by the need to generate and use knowledge; this depends both on the development of specialised pools of resources within administrative frameworks and on the organisation of trades relatively to one another – Marshall's first and third forms of organisation which aid knowledge.

Williamson's analysis, which, like Coase's, takes market contracting as its benchmark, assumes that vertical integration entails additional governance costs above those incurred in running separate but linked businesses, but that these costs are often lower than the costs created by opportunistic behaviour, or simply by the fear of such behaviour. Now we should distinguish between the transactions costs identified by Coase, which may be regarded, approximately, as natural, and those on which Williamson relies, an important part of which are man-made. Bounded rationality and information-impactedness, which greatly increase the scope for 'self-interest seeking with guile', as Williamson (1981, p. 1545) defines opportunism, are natural, though amendable; but it is the exploitation of these natural phenomena by those who ruthlessly seek their own advantage which causes the trouble; and the propensity to exploit is not a natural given.

Though Adam Smith (1976b, p. 145), as is well known, recognised the tendency for 'people of the same trade' to turn their conversation towards 'a conspiracy against the publick', he was also deeply impressed with the importance of conscience, as represented by 'the impartial spectator', as a regulator of conduct (Smith, 1976a, pp. 128-32). That he saw no inconsistency between moral sentiments and self-interest (which itself was far more sophisticated than simple greed) is demonstrated by the substantial revision of *The Theory of Moral Sentiments* which was published in 1790. The moral judgements which help to sustain society are formed in society (Smith, 1976a, pp. 110-12), and their effect on conduct decays with social or psychological distance: hence the importance of appeals to the self-interest rather than the benevolence of others in a highly specialised society.

This was another of Smith's themes which was taken up by Alfred Marshall, who was particularly concerned with 'the influence which the daily occupations of men exert on their character' (Marshall, 1975, p. 357). It was this influence which he chose to emphasise in the only existant report on his visit to America in 1875. The geographical and industrial mobility which characterised American industry, and the scope for ambition which it therefore offered, had consequences both good and bad. Americans were much less under the influence of custom and therefore more ready to strike out on new lines; on the other hand, the claims of a community of which one does not long expect to be a member are likely to be weak. 'Money is a more portable commodity than a high moral reputation ... . It cannot, I think, be denied that a short-sighted man is thus exposed to great temptations in America' (Marshall, 1975, p. 364).

It should therefore be no surprise that it has been an American economist who has systematically worked out the implications of opportunism for industrial organisation, nor that American economists have tended to construe rationality into an ever-stricter version of pure individual selfishness. But we may also conclude that firms which succeed in establishing an effective partnership to integrate activities which, though complementary, have very little in common, are likely to have a competitive advantage over those who are driven by fear of opportunism to bring such activities under a single management. Some evidence for such a competitive advantage has been provided by Casson (1990, pp. 105-24) in a comparison of American and Japanese industrial organisation, which is explained by the greater Japanese willingness to trust others, a product of their much more stable and homogeneous society. Trust between individuals or organisations allows each to draw on the reserves which are distributed within the trusting group.

There is a second likely reason for Williamson's oversimplification of the choice between markets and hierarchies. Not only does he give inadequate attention to the knowledge requirements of effective management; he has an inadequate conception of the institutions of the market. He praises (1986, p. 175) Llewellyn's (1931) assertion that 'the major importance of legal contract is to provide a framework for well-nigh every type of group organisation and for well-nigh every type of passing or permanent relations between individuals and groups ... a framework which almost never accurately indicates real working relations, but which affords a rough indication around which such relations vary', commenting 'This is a profoundly disturbing concept of contract.' It does not disturb him enough. It implies that market contracts, like the set of contracts which define a firm, are imperfectly specified, and need to be actively managed. As Demsetz (1988, p. 151) observes, 'the same organising activities often characterise exchange *and* management'.

Recognition of the uncertain consequences of contract, and the implications of bounded rationality, are crucial in determining the kinds of contract, or governance system, which are chosen; yet Williamson's adherence to the neoclassical research programme ensures that the impact of these uncertain consequences is exhausted in the choice which precedes them, precisely as in an Arrow-Debreu equilibrium.

The evolution of institutions, above all in ways which were not intended, plays no part in Williamson's analytical framework. He therefore gives inadequate attention to the possibilities and problems of managing market relationships, and to the variety of forms which these relationships may take. The distinction between markets and hierarchies is much less clear than he assumes: firms have internal markets, there may be cross-firm working arrangements, and sometimes part-ownership; and contracts both within and between firms may be implicitly renegotiated – at junior as well as senior levels.

Before Williamson developed his analysis, Richardson (1972, p. 884) had already pointed out that 'by looking at industrial reality in terms of a sharp dichotomy between firm and market we obtain a distorted view of how the system works'. By his use of the term 'external organisation' to describe a firm's network of contacts, Marshall (1920) had defined the management of this network as a normal business activity. The pure market contract is a limiting case (Richardson, 1972, p. 886): indeed relations between as well as within firms are typically governed by imperfectly specified contracts and tacit agreements (which, as Arrow (1974, p. 28) pointed out, may be among the hardest to break).

By defining the co-ordination problem in terms of a fixed list of goods and techniques, economists have ignored the need for qualitative co-ordination in the attempt to generate and use new knowledge (Richardson, 1972, p. 885). In accordance with Marshall's (1920, p. 241) general rule, quoted in Chapter 1, development requires both the refinement of specific expertise and its closer integration. This calls for an industrial organisation which operates somewhat like a scientific community, composed of rivalrous colleagues. Such an organisation requires the kind of equilibrium which can be provided by agreement on the connecting principles of theory and policy, in order to provide the framework, and the confidence, for evolution.

Market networks

The concept of a market as a set of complementary and competitive relationships (sometimes both together) is implicit in Richardson's work, as in Marshall's. It currently provides the framework of analysis for a group of Swedish economists, to which I shall do no more than draw attention (Mattson, 1987). Instead of the arm's length exchanges, regulated by carefully-specified contract, which are assumed in most economic models, firms may be linked, in pairs, or larger clusters, by a variety of continuing, though often intermittent technical, planning, social, or legal relationships, which evolve over time. People do not usually do business with strangers.

As Llewellyn pointed out, a contract provides a framework, and we should all recognise by now that some kind of framework is necessary for co-operation between either individuals or organisations; but a relationship which is governed strictly by the explicit terms of a contract will suffice for hardly any of the needs of business. It will cope neither with the detailed handling of production complementarities nor with the co-ordination of responses to changes in the market – which are never precisely foreseen, and like all events, need to be interpreted within some theoretical structure. As has been repeatedly discovered, it is not adequate (though it may often help) to accomplish the transfer of technology, because it is impossible to convey all the relevant knowledge in documents.

Firms invest in these relationships in the way that Marshall (1920) described, building up a complex structure of business capital, which may become essential, not only to their profitability, but even to their survival. A 'dense network of co-operation and affiliation' (Richardson, 1972, p. 883) provides each member with external reserves, and the flexibility of alternative pathways. Even if the internalisation of closely related activities increases the efficiency with which a firm can pursue a particular policy, it also imparts rigidity to that policy. Synergy is always paid for in degrees of freedom. We should not assume, however, that every relationship in such networks is deliberately crafted, to use a characteristic expression of Williamson; unintended consequences, both favourable and unfavourable, often leave their mark.

Reputation and goodwill are important in markets as in organisations – and among customers, suppliers, and rivals too. They are particularly important, as they are in scientific communities, when circumstances are changing, because new ideas, methods or products must initially be taken on trust. Casson (1990, p. 121), who has been steadily developing a theory of entrepreneurship which emphasises the importance of judgement based on simplified theories of complex environments, recognises the need for entrepreneurs to build a reputation which will allow them to create a market for their judgement.

Networks are characterised by Mattson in four ways: the degree of interdependence (complementary or competitive) between firms and the stability of network membership; the homogeneity of the pattern of relationships (for example, do all firms have similar links with their suppliers?); the degree of hierarchy in relationships (is dependence symmetrical, or does one party have a dominant influence?); and exclusiveness (to what extent are the members of this network prominent in other networks?). Analysis of the situation of a particular firm in these terms indicates the options available to it within the network, and what might be involved in creating new options.

Any attempt to explain the choices made must attempt to describe the network as envisaged by the relevant decision-makers, for this determines the perception of opportunities and constraints, not least through the information which is likely to be systematically sought. However, these perceptions, though subjective, are not incapable of analysis; the transactions within a network, whether this is a market, a firm, or a scientific community, both depend upon and generate shared assumptions about knowledge. How the shared assumption of continuous incremental change, based on a ceaseless flow of new technology, has made possible a highly successful blend of co-operation and competition in many Japanese industries is explained by Imai (1990). He emphasises its similarity to Marshall's 'knowledge growth mechanism' (1990, p. 196) and also its possible limitations.

If the existing framework is constricting, it is unlikely to be a good idea to try to do without a framework altogether. A promising strategy may then be to look for clusters of concepts, techniques, conventions or routines which seem to be effective in other networks, and to attempt to create a new assembly of viable sub-systems. Such a strategy may be followed in both business and in science – where it offers a solution to the mystery in Kuhn's theory of scientific revolution: where does a new paradigm come from?

Vertical relationships and alliances may be particularly attractive if a company wishes to challenge the established theories, policies, and routines of a market – if the market equilibrium seems to impede the kind of evolution that the company wishes to pursue. For example, if every car distributor is linked to, and dependent on, a manufacturer, and the population of distributors is stable, entry by a new manufacturer is difficult; but such a new manufacturer might seek to create a new network by linking up with a chain of superstores. It should recognise, however, that such a strategy is likely to make the firm less acceptable to any distributor who might become available thereafter. To achieve any major innovation it is necessary to build a coalition; and effective coalitions are quasi-decomposable systems. Participants in a market, or in related markets, may also form coalitions to resist change, as Schumpeter (1934, pp. 86-7) observed; that was one reason why entrepreneurs in his theory have to be tough, and not too concerned about the feelings or indeed the fortunes of other people.

The management of market relationships is, I suggest, the most neglected topic in the whole of economics. The reason for this neglect is very simple: it is a topic which cannot be comfortably accommodated within the network of theories and policies which are shared by the great majority of economists, and which support the reliability of economic knowledge. It requires an alternative network, which nevertheless does not discard every element which is familiar. The development of such a network is the strategy that I have been using in this book, a policy for creating a theory to sustain a new equilibrium of knowledge-generating activities.

6

Innovation

Organisation and innovation

How to organise for innovation is a popular topic among writers on organisation, and it seems to be widely agreed that tightly disciplined structures are not appropriate. So much is implied in the distinction between improvements and innovation which has been made in a recent article by a senior manager in IBM. Improvement is there defined as 'a change taking place within a system ... an improvement normally involves only one function, perhaps even a single department'; improvements, we may say, are strictly constrained by the theory and policy which define a sub-system equilibrium. Those constraints, however, are violated by innovation. 'Breaking the rules is, indeed, what principally characterises innovation ... innovation normally implies moving outside the logic of the system' (Grossi, 1990, p. 43). What Grossi calls the logic of the system is embodied in its theories and policies; his definition therefore precisely fits the interpretative framework employed in this book.

Conventional rules of organisation lead to highly decomposed structures, in which tasks are clearly specified and performance closely monitored, thus apparently solving the principal-agent problem. The need to break such rules, if innovation is to be made possible, was emphasised by Burns and Stalker (1961) in their study of the attempts by Scottish engineering companies to diversify into electronics. The theories and policies of these firms had proved highly compatible with a stable technology in a stable environment, in which firms had chosen (to use Kelly's (1963, p. 65) terminology) to constrict their vision in order to define it more precisely. By limiting each person's discretion, and thus the realm of relevant facts (Kelly, 1963, pp. 8-9), they had ensured predictability, simplified decision-making and achieved the static efficiency which a 'mechanistic' system can produce.

Innovation, by contrast, required new connections, and could not succeed unless people were prepared to broaden their vision and tolerate the uncertainties which are inevitably created by following problems across conventional boundaries. Since the relevant interactions could not be defined in advance, and indeed varied over time, it was not possible simply to respecify the principles of decomposition. Burns and Stalker argued that the most effective response was to create an 'organic', or self-organising system, in which people would be free to create and dissolve appropriate working relationships to fit the changing needs of each innovative project.

The coherence of such an evolving network could not be achieved by formal hierarchies or conventional systems of management control, but only by securing a strong commitment to the organisation as a whole, and therefore to theories and policies (as we may plausibly interpret Arrow's (1974, p. 72) phrase 'convergent expectations') which were capable of sustaining its equilibrium while it developed new products for new markets. In most of the firms studied, this commitment was not forthcoming; the old sub-system theories and policies proved almost impervious to new messages. In Schumpeter's (1934, p. 80) phrase, things had had ample 'time to hammer logic into men', and the confrontation between this impermeable logic and the novel technological and business environment produced precisely the kind of crises that Kelly wished to understand.

This contrast between the efficient decomposition of a system which is fully adjusted to well-established knowledge, like the orthodox models of a perfectly competitive economy, and the kind of poorly-defined relationships which encourage people to break conventional rules and escape the logic which flows inexorably from outdated premises, keeps reappearing in later work. Klein (1977) associates rapid economic growth with the innovative success of 'organised disorganisation', which encourages random communications between diverse people who are trying by a variety of means to reach an agreed objective. Peters and Waterman (1982) claim that excellent companies encourage a variety of experiments, initiated and appraised by informal groups, while maintaining coherence by creating a powerful, even rigid, corporate culture. Their observation (p. 116) that almost no big innovation is used as was originally intended carries a strong warning against attempts at programming. In writing of the need for 'core values' (p. 15), they unconsciously but quite properly recall Lakatos' hard core, which is essential to the cohesion of a loosely-structured group trying to advance knowledge by collaborating and competing within a shared research programme. Kanter (1984) echoes Burns and Stalker's contrast between segmentation, to facilitate predictability and control, and integration, to encourage enterprise and the unpredictability of new ideas.

Though much of Williamson's analysis, which was discussed in the previous chapter, is based on the assumption that people will supplement self-interest with guile whenever they have the opportunity, he does recognise the great advantages of shared objectives and attitudes when human assets are highly specific to the organisation and contributions to effective performance are not readily separable (Williamson, 1985, p. 247). If these objectives and attitudes are supported by a relevant and amendable framework of business-related knowledge they can provide a promising setting for innovation. The proviso is important; such closely-integrated groups may also coalesce around traditional values and impede change. The Japanese preference for loosely-defined organisational structures, noted in the previous chapter, seems particularly appropriate to the lengthy process of detailed improvement which, as Pavitt (1987, pp. 124-5) observes, is usually necessary before an innovation becomes clearly superior to the products or processes which it challenges.

Innovative systems

Organisational coherence, as we have seen, requires powerful constraints of some kind; not all rules can be broken at any one time if the firm is not to disintegrate. But there remains the possibility of achieving variety across rival firms pursuing different research programmes, following different policies, and judging events by different criteria. We should not overlook the danger that business schools, consultants, writers on management, and financial institutions could produce too much uniformity of approach. Even studies of innovation which compare alternative

approaches may give too much attention to identifying gui-
delines for success at the expense of exploring the advantages of
diversity. Financial institutions, indeed, have shown a strong
tendency to adopt similar theories and policies for their own
businesses, which have unfortunately evoked strong messages
suggesting the need for revision. It therefore seems no less im-
portant than when Schumpeter wrote to leave room for out-
siders.

Outsiders may, of course, be migrants from another industry,
transferring a research programme from one context to another,
and opening up new lines of inquiry. The realisation of this
possibility is well recognised in scientific research; it appears to
be quite common in business. Firms may attempt to introduce
new marketing policies, technologies, or operating procedures
which resemble those apparently employed by other firms, either
because their interpretative frameworks are permeable to outside
influences, or – especially in a crisis – on the assumption that
someone else has a better policy. Other firms, whose current
policies appear to have been successful in their present environ-
ment, may seek to apply them in other market areas. Either trans-
fer, of course, may fail.

On the basis of the analysis, not only of this chapter but of the
whole book, one would expect innovations, which defy the logic
of the system, to be predominantly the work of people who have
not become habituated to the current theories and policies of the
firm and market which the innovation would change or bypass.
Such people are more likely to have access to alternative theories
and policies, and be less likely to be deterred by the apparent
consequences of accepting the refutation of large parts of the pre-
valent research programme. Indeed, if they have made no com-
mitment to that research programme, they may see substantial
personal advantages in its displacement. The argument was
clearly made by Marshall (1920, p. 197), in almost equivalent
terms.

The expectation is well-corroborated: innovations often come
from outsiders. The Britten-Norman Islander, a simple, rugged
aircraft with a high wing, fixed undercarriage, and rectangular
body section to maximise the usable interior space, was well-cal-
culated to solve the problems which its British designers had en-
countered during years of flying experience in third-world

countries; an American engineer, who had worked in the US aircraft industry, assured me that no such aircraft could ever have been conceived by an American designer, since it violated the accepted conventions of modern design, which had been tested against the very different institutions of the US market. Britten and Norman were, unfortunately, less successful in creating a viable policy for profitable manufacture than in designing an aircraft which has met a substantial demand, and the Islander is now produced by a Swiss company.

Hannah (1984) has drawn attention to the continuing prominence of immigrants among the builders of successful British businesses; and surely no one was surprised by Casson's (1982) choice of a typical entrepreneur. A fascinating example, from the immigrant's point of view, of how easily different frameworks of thought lead to different policies is provided by Pasold's (1977) account of the development of the Ladybird clothing business in Britain – an account which might now be effectively, but regrettably, counterpointed by the story of its decline in the hands of its British buyers, who did not understand flair, but proposed to replace this by efficient administration (Pasold, 1977, p. 654).

The environment of innovation

Innovations always change the systems into which they are introduced. They disrupt established theories and policies, and violate the principles on which those systems have been decomposed into quasi-isolated sub-systems. They require the creation of new theories and policies, and new schemes of decomposition. They begin by changing the firm which introduces them (unless they are incorporated into a new firm), and may fail if the firm's theories and policies are recalcitrant, as they were in the study by Burns and Stalker (1961). A common device for circumventing recalcitrance is to move to another location, as Ford once moved from Manchester to Dagenham and, more recently, W. H. Smith their book and stationery warehouse from London to Swindon: my judgement is that the latter move, or some equivalent, was an inescapable condition of achieving the changes which the firm sought, and probably needed in order to survive (Loasby, 1973). Both companies, it will be noted, moved into areas where there was no relevant tradition. Similarly, Pasold resolved not to locate in or around Nottingham, and chose Slough: the external economies of established knitwear centres provided a constricting institutional framework which he was determined to avoid. Nissan and Toyota have likewise kept away from established centres of car manufacture in Britain.

If a satisfactory system for delivering the innovation can be achieved, there remains the problem of introducing it into the external network. Innovations may fail because they are too timid, or because they are too far-reaching. The policies, and comparative successes, of the Stephensons and the Brunels are worth considering from this point of view. (George Stephenson, like his father, was employed by Northumbrian coal-owners, in an area where waggonways were well established; the elder Brunel was born in France, where he received a sound technical education, and also spent some time in America.) Compatibility with existing practices, procedures, and ways of thinking, is as important an issue in the market network as in the innovating organisation.

Loose-coupling often appears to be a disadvantage to those who are seeking to implement major changes which require, as they usually do, the active co-operation of others – though one should not forget that innovations, like new scientific ideas, often need to be sheltered from external criticism for a time. A successful innovation requires an effective coalition – which is a useful way to think about marketing strategy. The research programmes of the participants will be different, for they provide the theories and policies appropriate to their particular specialisations; but those specialisations must be closely connected, by appropriate links of thought and incentive.

These issues are not always adequately considered, as three examples may show. The attempts by the National Engineering Laboratory to promote the use of cold forming ignored the implications for engineering shops of inserting into the production flow a mechanical operation which required chemical treatment of the workpiece both before and after. This would have created crucial interdependencies, both of technology and of inter-union relations, which few such businesses had any basis for handling, and which were therefore best avoided.

Mond Division of ICI assigned the US market for a new fire-fighting powder to the American market leader in fire-fighting equipment, confident that this arrangement assured success, and did not welcome the opinion that it would be disastrous; as it was. Since the new powder was five times as effective as its predecessor, it required much smaller apparatus; and most of the profit is made on the apparatus. The American company already supplied over half the market; so what Mond was offering was the prospect of a substantial reduction in profit. It was also, unwittingly, offering the power to block the threat; and the American company was willing to pay something to prevent the new powder being offered to a smaller competitor, for whom the reduced profit per unit might easily be outweighed by gain in market share.

The third example is of widespread misjudgement among companies within a shared institutional framework – the fashion for joint ventures between American computer companies and publishers in the 1960s, which were intended to exploit the supposedly huge potential market for programmed learning. These conjectures were falsified by the incompatibility between the extent of standardisation required to bring down costs and the local autonomy which characterised the American education industry. Courses could not be sold like Model T Fords, or personal computers.

If the network is not receptive, one possibility may be to internalise part of it, as Courtaulds did in order to develop the market for their fibres. It is possible to construe such a move as an example of vertical integration to reduce transactions costs, by focusing on the difficulty of writing a contract which would adequately specify the operating practices, and the knowledge, required of the downstream partner; but it may be better to consider directly the problems of achieving compatibility. Can practices and assumptions be aligned across a market boundary? Can they be aligned better within a single organisation, without destroying the compatibility between the newly-acquired business and its customers? In the process of securing increased attention for one's own products by the firm taken over, may one damage that firm's ability to market effectively at the next stage?

As Casson (1990, p. 38) reminds us, the internalisation of the linkage on which attention is focussed is likely to carry with it the internalisation of many other linkages which may pose unwanted, and sometimes intractable, problems. A focus on transactions costs is likely to pre-empt adequate consideration of the effects of vertical integration on relations between other members of the network. Many firms are very wary of any action which might be interpreted as competing with their customers, if these customers have access to alternative sources of supply. Their attitude may be misconceived, but one should seek to understand the institutional pattern which encourages the conception.

Evolution and innovation in market systems

Market networks, and the routines which support them, were discussed in the previous chapter. Like the routines which characterise a firm, market routines are likely to drift over time, in large part for similar reasons. Incremental changes in technology may increase or reduce the relative importance of particular complementary links; an equally-balanced relationship may gradually turn in favour of one party; changes in demand, consequent on changes in income, may create interdependencies between previously separate networks.

The evolution of market institutions may lead to consequences quite outside the intentions of those who helped to create them. A striking and important example has been given by Hannah (1984, p. 225): tax relief for insurance premiums, which was introduced by Gladstone to encourage entrepreneurs by reducing the cost of protecting their family's income, has helped to encourage a pattern of institutionalised saving which has diverted funds away from entrepreneurs. I would like to conclude this chapter by sketching two case histories, which illustrate the general principle that discontinuities are linked to continuities; the successful entrepreneur knows (or happens to guess right) which rules to observe, as well as which rules to break.

Economists compound their neglect of the internal operation of a firm by collapsing the sequence of product markets into a single stage: producers buy factor services (even materials are liable to be forgotten) and sell to consumers. But the sequential structure is important, especially if we are studying fixprice markets. Who sets prices along the chain? Why, and with what consequences?

Let us consider the relationship between manufacturer and retailer. The decline of the merchants in the late nineteenth century was the obverse of the increasing power of the manufacturer, who became the price-setter, not only at the factory gate, but also in the retail shop. Why the manufacturer should wish to set the retailer's prices is not hard to explain: without the ability to determine prices, the scope of any marketing strategy is likely to be seriously limited. In particular, if a manufacturer wished to have his full range widely carried and actively sold, he needed to offer his stockists a good profit margin, and to protect that margin from undercutting by competitors who might aim for a quick turnover on a narrow range. An additional inducement to carry a large range, parts of which might be slow-selling, was provided by offering generous credit. (No doubt this can also be explained on efficiency grounds: the larger manufacturers, at least, could presumably borrow on easier terms than almost all retailers.)

For most retailers, this was probably a very satisfactory policy: it provided them with an elaborate institutional framework within which to employ their particular skills in display, personal service (including delivery), and the granting of credit. It clearly suited the co-operative stores (then growing in importance) very well indeed, for the prices of their own-brand products were kept in line with the prices of similar goods in private shops; the high margins thus made possible were reflected in generous patronage dividends (10 per cent or more was common for many years) which held their customers and also encouraged them to save – a service for which the co-operative movement has perhaps not received enough recognition.

After 1945 the pattern began to change. The increasing range of goods demanded in grocers' shops made counter service increasingly inefficient as, with the rise in shop assistants' wages, it was also becoming more expensive. Self-service offered an answer. The initiative was taken by co-operative stores, which generally had larger floor-areas and provided slower counter service; the greater loyalty of their customers (partly attributable to the patronage dividend) reduced the apparent risk of the experiment (McClelland, 1963, p. 20).

Self-service had two important consequences. It offered economies of scale, one element of which was an economy of stocks, and thus encouraged expansion; it also, as the practice became common, removed the distinction between shops in the quality of personal services. A new productive opportunity emerged, which took the form of supermarket chains. Price-cutting was an obvious means of attracting customers, and also, at first, a distinctive policy. 'Pile it high and sell it cheap' (the slogan of Tesco's founder) if not quite sufficient to define a marketing strategy, was certainly an effective paradigm or research programme.

Manufacturers resisted the attack on resale price maintenance, because of the implications for their own strategy, and so did the small shopkeepers, for whom price-cutting was not attractive; but both groups were gradually losing power to the customer appeal of price-cutting supermarkets. Retail co-operatives also suffered, because price-cutting undermined their distinctive institution of a substantial patronage dividend; their introduction of self-service affords one of the most striking examples of actions having consequences which formed no part of the actors' intentions.

Manufacturers unintentionally accelerated their loss of power by seizing two business opportunities. One was the manufacture of goods to be sold under the retailer's label, which circumvented the dispute over resale price maintenance and also helped to give the self-service retailer an identity. As Drucker (1964, p. 100) points out, 'a store whose reputation rests exclusively on the brand names everybody else can carry has no reputation or identity at all. All it has is an address.' But the retailer's identity is gained at the manufacturer's expense; for it is not easy for a manufacturer to keep control over a product which carries the retailer's label. The brand policy is the retailer's: he has a wide sphere of initiative, if he can use it. Kellogg's persistent refusal to make own-label products is entirely understandable.

The second opportunity was presented by the rapid growth of supermarkets, especially the Fine Fare chain, well in advance of the management skills needed to operate this new kind of retail store. Lever Brothers (and no doubt many other manufacturers) perceived a prospect of gaining business by supplying what most store managers lacked – skills in merchandising and stock control. In dealing with supermarkets they therefore switched from 'selling in' to 'selling out': instead of trying to persuade the manager to increase his order, the salesman now worked out a stock control scheme which specified reorder points and order quantities, while the merchandiser who accompanied him was giving advice on store layout – with particular attention, naturally, to the display of Lever's products. This was no doubt a good policy in the circumstances; but once the skills were transferred Lever Brothers, and other suppliers, had lost more degrees of freedom.

Perhaps of even greater interest is the way in which one of the market routines which had helped manufacturers to gain control now helped them to lose it. Most modern retailers (not just supermarkets) aim to turn over stock very quickly; yet they still receive generous credit from their suppliers – often for a longer period than the goods remain unsold. They also sell for cash. Supermarket chains have negative current assets. (If VAT were extended to foodstuffs, the present collection routines would deluge them with even more cash.) It is thus far easier to finance the expansion of a quick-turnover retail business than that of manufacturer. We should not therefore be surprised to find retailing so much more attractive to entrepreneurs.

The market routines have clearly been working in favour of entrepreneurial retail businesses. Not only has the increasing concentration of ownership given them formidable bargaining power; they have now taken control of most of the principal components of marketing. It is increasingly difficult for manufacturers to gain access to customers except on their terms. In this transformed setting, the available options for all members of the network are very different from what they used to be. One important change is that most major retail chains provide a simpler route to the British market for overseas suppliers than is available for British firms in many foreign markets.

For a final example, we may consider the drift of market routines which provided the opportunity for the rapid growth of a retail service business, Kwikfit Euro. The need for both frequent regular servicing and a substantial incidence of repairs and replacement had indicated the efficiency of combining car maintenance with dealership; and this arrangement also provided manufacturers with at least the chance of better information about the durability and defects of their products, and some control over the treatment which they received from motor mechanics.

But as service intervals and reliability improved, the replacement of tyres, batteries and silencers gradually became more prominent: being less likely to coincide with any other repair or servicing need, each could be debited with the loss of the car for a day, at a cost which reflected the overheads of an all-purpose garage. There was a marketing opportunity for a new business policy, based on an updated theory of this market: a centre specially designed to accommodate the limited routines necessary to provide these three services quickly, while the customer waited, within a building and organisation in which simplicity and ease of control facilitated both quality and low overheads. Indeed, as Tom Farmer, the founder of Kwikfit Euro, recognised, simplicity and ease of control, enhanced by effective use of communication by computer, favoured a chain of such centres, with its consequent buying power.

The creation of this new business was powerfully assisted by the perpetuation of a routine equivalent to that from which the supermarkets benefited. Generous credit was not a rule to be broken, because it prevented financial constraints on growth. Provided that the service offered was good enough and fast enough to keep the customers coming, growth was automatically financed by the suppliers. Though Farmer's rate of stockturn was slower than a supermarket's the customary credit period was longer. By fitting, for cash, within a month tyres and silencers which were sold on three months' credit (or more, as the tyre companies became increasingly desperate for outlets), he had the use of the money for two months, interest-free; and the faster the business grew, the more cash it made available. The star was also a cash cow.

One must wonder whether the resultant structure is stable. Can the combination of dealer and full-service garage, deprived of its most profitable business and left with its overheads, survive? In whose interests is it that car sales should still be linked with service? The framework for business decisions in this industry have changed. There is scope for new theories and new policies, which are likely to produce, by design or unanticipated consequence, further changes in routines and networks, within and between firms.

7

Conclusion

The economic problem is the co-ordination of economic activities; and co-ordination is needed because specialisation is more productive than self-sufficiency. That is pure orthodoxy, and I endorse it. But the co-ordination problem is not that defined by Jevons, and repeated in introductory textbooks: the allocation of known resources, with known properties, to known possibilities of production and consumption. Even that is not a simple task, and neoclassical theory still cannot tell us how it is to be done. But the more difficult, and continually changing problem, is that of co-ordinating the growth of knowledge. Here, too, specialisation is more productive, but only if the specialists are effectively co-ordinated. But future knowledge cannot be known before it has been invented, so neither rational choice nor equilibrium can be defined as they have come to be defined in neoclassical economics. Moreover, the price mechanism is not sufficient for co-ordinating closely complementary activities, such as those of economists working on international trade theory, or businesses working on the development and use of new materials.

The co-ordination of these activities depends on rational structures and rational procedures rather than rational choice. Developing economies, like developing sciences, need systems which are stable enough to give confidence to the people working within them to develop and try out new ideas, which can then be appraised, tested, and, if successful, used within those systems. The conditions under which such systems are stable can be treated as a problem of equilibrium: one condition is that they should be capable of internal flexibility. That, by an extension of Coase's (1937) explanation for the existence of firms, implies imperfectly-specified contracts – indeed often tacit contracts, or invisible handshakes, and even some deliberate ambiguity. Firms and markets, as well as scientific communities, are learning systems – a concept which some organisations have recently adopted. That is the direction in which Shell has been moving, guided by its experience with scenarios. Imperfectly-specified contracts, frameworks, paradigms, or research programmes, create space in which people can invent, imagine, and explore possible futures, between which they or others can later choose. They constitute what Eliasson (1987) has called 'an experimentally organised economy'.

This process requires the tolerance of a good deal of inconsistency, which may be assisted by insulating different groups. Insulation is facilitated by decomposability – the decomposition of the economy into quasi-isolated industries and markets, the decomposition of industries and markets into sectors which differ in their conceptions of what customers would want and how these wants might be met, the decomposition of sectors into organisations which devise and examine variants of products and processes, and the decomposition of firms into divisions, then departments, then working groups.

At every level we might try as a general theme – an imperfectly specified research strategy – Burton Klein's (1977) proposition that micro-stability undermines macro-stability; though I suggest we also remember that decomposability is never complete, and that local flexibility may have wide ramifications, perhaps long-delayed, and probably unexpected. However, differences between divisions, firms and industries in the ways they search for knowledge not only increases the scope of that search: it also develops a variety of expertise which can provide some provision for coping with unexpected discontinuities. Adaptation can occur at several levels; what is possible at each level may depend on the institutions which operate there.

Monitoring and anticipating such effects is most obviously the responsibility of senior management, and the proper objective of long-range planning (as I am surprised to find that I said in an article (Loasby, 1967) published over twenty years ago but which has recently found favour with a leading writer on management); yet there are other ways of trying to do this, by encouraging direct contacts between those members of sub-systems who are directly engaged in generating new knowledge. Such patterns of behaviour are recommended in some modern writing on management, as we have seen; on the argument of this book, they require a different kind of high-level framework, which will impose system-wide constraints without causing them to be resented – perhaps what Schumpeter calls a vision.

Does this conception of the co-ordination problem make prediction impossible? I don't think so; I have even offered a prediction or two – some more conjectural than others – in the course of this book. What is more likely to be predictable is system behaviour and its consequences – just as in orthodox economics. And even though future knowledge cannot be predicted if it is to remain *future* knowledge, it may often be possible to set limits on it – to say what cannot be done. Even that kind of prediction may be wrong, because, let us remember, there is no way of proving any general proposition to be true. In the face of that fundamental obstacle, we have perhaps not done too badly.

A good economist, in my view, is someone who has a difficulty for every solution; so let me leave readers with a problem. It is an underlying theme of this book that different structures and different procedures lead to different results – in particular, to different kinds of knowledge. My problem is this; are these different kinds of knowledge all way-stations along different routes to some unique final truth? Is the growth of knowledge ultimately governed by path-dependency or equifinality? I know what my theory is, and it is a theory which will defy unwelcome messages from the economy or anywhere else; for I refuse to believe that, in the end, none of this matters, and that we have all been wasting our time.

References

Ansoff, H. I. (1965), *Corporate Strategy*, McGraw-Hill, New York.

Argyris, C. (1985), *Strategy, Change and Defensive Routines*, Ballinger, Cambridge, MA.

Arrow, K. J. (1974), *The Limits of Organization*, W. W. Norton, New York.

Becker, G. (1976), *The Economic Approach to Human Behavior*, University of Chicago Press, Chicago.

Blaug, M. (1980), *The Methodology of Economics*, Cambridge University Press, Cambridge.

Burns, T. and Stalker, G. M. (1961), *The Management of Innovation*, Tavistock, London.

Casson, M. (1982), *The Entrepreneur: An Economic Theory*, Martin Robertson, Oxford.

Casson, M. (1990), *Enterprise and Competitiveness: A Systems View of International Business*, Clarendon Press, Oxford.

Chamberlin, E. H. (1933), *The Theory of Monopolistic Competition*, Harvard University Press, Cambridge, MA.

Chandler, A. D. (1962), *Strategy and Structure*, MIT Press, Cambridge, MA.

Coase, R. H. (1937), 'The nature of the firm', *Economica*, N.S.4, pp. 386-405. Reprinted in Coase (1988), pp. 33-55.

Coase, R. H. (1972), 'Industrial organizations: a proposal for research', in Fuchs, V. R. (ed.), *Policy Issues and Research Opportunities in Industrial Organization*, National Bureau of Economic Research, New York, pp. 59-73. Reprinted in Coase (1988), pp. 57-74.

Coase, R. H. (1988), *The Firm, the Market, and the Law*, University of Chicago Press, Chicago.

Coddington, A. (1975), 'The rationale of general equilibrium theory', *Economic Inquiry*, XIII, pp. 539-58.

Cyert, R. M. and March, J. G. (1963), *A Behavioral Theory of the Firm*, Prentice-Hall, Englewood Cliffs, NJ.

Demsetz, H. (1988), *The Organization of Economic Activity, Volume I: Ownership, Control, and the Firm*, Basil Blackwell, Oxford.

Dosi, G. (1982), 'Technological paradigms and technological trajectories', *Research Policy*, 11, pp. 147-62.

Drucker, P. F. (1955), *The Practice of Management*, Heinemann, London.

Drucker, P. F. (1964), *Managing for Results*, Heinemann, London.

Earl, P. E. (1984), *The Corporate Imagination: How Big Companies Make Mistakes*, Wheatsheaf, Brighton, and M. E. Sharpe, Armonk, NY.

Eliasson, G. (1987), *Technological Competition and Trade in the Experimentally Organized Economy*, IUI Research Report no.32, IUI, Stockholm.

Eliasson, G. (1991), 'Deregulation, innovative entry and structured diversity as a source of stable and rapid economic growth', *Journal of Evolutionary Economics*, 1, 1, pp. 49-63.

Foster, R. (1986), *Innovation: the Attacker's Advantage*, Macmillan, London.

Goold, M. and Campbell, A. (1987), *Strategies and Styles: The Role of the Centre in Managing Diversified Corporations*, Basil Blackwell, Oxford.

Graham, M. B. W. (1986), *The Business of Research: RCA and the Videodisc*, Cambridge University Press, Cambridge.

Grossi, G. (1990), 'Promoting innovation in a big business', *Long Range Planning*, 23, 1, pp. 41-52.

Hahn, F. H. (1973), *On the Notion of Equilibrium in Economics*, Cambridge University Press, Cambridge. Reprinted in Hahn (1984), pp. 43-71.

Hahn, F. H. (1984), *Equilibrium and Macroeconomics*, Basil Blackwell, Oxford.

Hahn, F. H. (1991), 'The next hundred years', *Economic Journal*, 101, pp. 47-50.

Hannah, L. (1984), 'Entrepreneurs and the social sciences', *Economica*, 51, pp. 219-34.

Hayek, F. A. (1931), *Prices and Production*, Routledge, London.

Hayek, F. A. (1937), 'Economics and knowledge', *Economica*, 4, pp. 33-54. Reprinted in Hayek (1948), pp. 33-56.

Hayek, F. A. (1946), 'The meaning of competition', Stafford Little Lecture, Princeton University. Reprinted in Hayek (1948), pp. 92-106.

Hayek, F. A. (1948), *Individualism and Economic Order*, University of Chicago Press, Chicago.

Heiner, R. A. (1983), 'The origin of predictable behavior', *American Economic Review*, 75, pp. 560-95.

Hicks, J. R. (1982), *Collected Essays on Economic Theory. Volume II: Money, Interest and Wages*, Basil Blackwell, Oxford.

Hirschman, A. O. (1970), *Exit, Voice and Loyalty*, Harvard University Press, Cambridge, MA.

Imai, K. J. (1990), 'Patterns of innovation and entrepreneurship in Japan', in Heertje, A. and Perlman, M., *Evolving Technology and Market Structure: Studies in Schumpeterian Economics*, University of Michigan Press, Ann Arbor, MI.

Jevons, W. S. (1871), *The Theory of Political Economy*, Macmillan, London and New York.

Kanter, R. M. (1984), *The Change Masters: Corporate Entrepreneurs at Work*, Allen and Unwin, London.

Kelly, G. A. (1963), *A Theory of Personality*, W. W. Norton, New York.

Keynes, J. M. (1936), *The General Theory of Employment, Interest and Money*, Macmillan, London.

Kirzner, I. M. (1973), *Competition and Entrepreneurship*, University of Chicago Press, Chicago.

Klein, B. (1977), *Dynamic Economics*, Harvard University Press, Cambridge, MA.

Kuhn, T. S. (1962, 1970), *The Structure of Scientific Revolutions*, University of Chicago Press, Chicago.

Lachmann, L. M. (1986), *The Market as an Economic Process*, Basil Blackwell, Oxford.

Lakatos, I. (1970), 'Falsification and the methodology of scientific research programmes' in Lakatos, I. and Musgrave, A. (eds.), *Criticism and the Growth of Knowledge*, Cambridge University Press, Cambridge, pp. 91-195.

Llewellyn, K. N. (1931), 'What price contract? - an essay in perspective', *Yale Law Journal*, 40, pp. 704-51.

Loasby, B. J. (1967), 'Long range formal planning in perspective', *Journal of Management Studies*, 4, 3, pp. 300-8.

Loasby, B. J. (1973), *The Swindon Project*, Pitman, London.

Loasby, B. J. (1976), *Choice, Complexity and Ignorance*, Cambridge University Press, Cambridge.

Loasby, B. J. (1989), *The Mind and Method of the Economist*, Edward Elgar, Aldershot.

Loasby, B. J. (1990), 'The use of scenarios in business planning', in Frowen, S. F. (ed.), *Unknowledge and Choice in Economics*, Macmillan, Basingstoke, pp. 46-63.

McClelland, W. G. (1963), *Studies in Retailing*, Basil Blackwell, Oxford.

Marris, R. L. (1964), *The Economic Theory of 'Managerial' Capitalism*, Macmillan, London.

Marshall, A. (1919), *Industry and Trade*, Macmillan, London.

Marshall, A. (1920), *Principles of Economics*, 8th edn, Macmillan, London.

Marshall, A. (1975), 'Some features of American Industry', in Whitaker, J. K. (ed.), *The Early Economic Writings of Alfred Marshall 1867-1890*, Vol. 2, Macmillan, London, pp. 355-77.

Masterman, M. (1970), 'The nature of a paradigm', in Lakatos, I. and Musgrave, A. (eds.), *Criticism and the Growth of Knowledge*, Cambridge University Press, Cambridge, pp. 59-88.

Mattson, L. G. (1987), 'Management of strategic change in a "Markets-as-Networks" perspective', in Pettigrew (1987), pp. 234-56.

Melin, L. (1987), 'Commentary', on Grant, R. M., 'Business change and strategy change in a hostile environment: failure and success among British cutlery producers', in Pettigrew (1987), pp. 154-65.

Menger, C. (1871 [1950]), *Principles of Economics*, translated by Dingwall, J. and Hoselitz, B. F., Free Press, Glencoe, IL.

Metcalfe, J. S. and Boden, M. (1990), 'Strategy, paradigm and evolutionary change'. Paper presented to Conference on Corporate Strategy and Technical Change, University of Manchester, to be published in Coombs, R., Saviotti, P. and Walsh, V., *Technological Change and Corporate Strategy: Economic and Sociological Perspectives*, Academic Press, London, 1992.

Nelson, R. R. and Winter, S. G. (1982), *An Evolutionary Theory of Economic Change*, Harvard University Press, Cambridge, MA.

O'Driscoll, G. P. Jr and Rizzo, M. (1985), *The Economics of Time and Ignorance*, Basil Blackwell, Oxford.

Pasold, E. (1977), *Ladybird, Ladybird*, Manchester University Press, Manchester.

Pavitt, K. (1987), 'Commentary' on Tushman, M. and Anderson, P., 'Technological discontinuities and organization environments', in Pettigrew (1987), pp. 123-7.

Penrose, E. T. (1959), *The Theory of the Growth of the Firm*, Oxford University Press, Oxford.

Peters, T. J. and Waterman, R. H. (1982), *In Search of Excellence*, Harper and Row, New York.

Pettigrew, A. M. (ed.) (1987), *The Management of Strategic Change*, Basil Blackwell, Oxford.

Pfeffer, J. and Salancik, G. R. (1978), *The External Control of Organisations*, Harper and Row, New York.

Popper, K. R. (1972), *The Logic of Scientific Discovery*, 6th impression, Hutchinson, London.

Reder, M. W. (1982), 'Chicago economics: permanence and change', *Journal of Economic Literature*, XX, pp. 1-38.

Richardson, G. B. (1960), *Information and Investment*, Oxford University Press, Oxford.

Richardson, G. B. (1990), *Information and Investment*, with new foreword, introduction and additional chapters, Clarendon Press, Oxford.

Richardson, G. B. (1972), 'The organisation of industry', *Economic Journal*, 82, pp. 883-96. Reprinted in Richardson (1990), pp. 224-42.

Richardson, G. B. (1975), 'Adam Smith on competition and increasing returns' in Skinner, A. S. and Wilson, T. (eds.), *Essays on Adam Smith*, Oxford University Press, Oxford.

Robertson, D. H. (1952), *Utility and All That and Other Essays*, Allen and Unwin, London.

Robinson, J. V. (1933), *The Economics of Imperfect Competition*, Macmillan, London.

Robinson, R. (1971), *Edward H. Chamberlin*, Columbia University Press, New York and London.

Rogers, K. (1963), *Managers: Personality and Performance*, Tavistock, London.

Samuelson, P. A. (1967), 'The monopolistic competition revolution', in Kuenne, R. E. (ed.), *Monopolistic Competition: Studies in Impact*, Wiley, New York. Reprinted in Merton, R. K. (ed.), *The Collected Scientific Papers of Paul A. Samuelson*, Vol. 2, MIT

Press, Cambridge, MA and London, pp. 18-51. (Reference is to this reprint.)

Schumpeter, J. A. (1934), *The Theory of Economic Development*, Harvard University Press, Cambridge, MA.

Schumpeter, J. A. (1943), *Capitalism, Socialism and Democracy*, Allen and Unwin, London.

Shackle, G. L. S. (1967, 1983), *The Years of High Theory: Invention and Tradition in Economic Thought 1926-1939*, Cambridge University Press, Cambridge.

Shackle, G. L. S. (1972), *Epistemics and Economics*, Cambridge University Press, Cambridge.

Simon, H. A. (1965), *The Shape of Automation for Men and Management*, Harper and Row, New York.

Simon, H. A. (1969), *The Sciences of the Artificial*, MIT Press, Cambridge, MA.

Simon, H. A. (1982), *Models of Bounded Rationality*, 2 vols., MIT Press, Cambridge, MA.

Smith, A. (1976a), *The Theory of Moral Sentiments*, ed. Raphael, D. D. and Macfie, A. L., Oxford University Press, Oxford.

Smith, A. (1976b), *An Inquiry into the Nature and Causes of the Wealth of Nations*, ed. Campbell, R. H., Skinner, A. S. and Todd, W. B., 2 vols., Oxford University Press, Oxford.

Smith, A. (1980), 'The principles which lead and direct philosophical enquiries: illustrated by the history of astronomy' in Wightman, W. P. D. (ed.), *Essays on Philosophical Subjects* (1795), Oxford University Press, Oxford, pp. 33-105.

Sraffa, P. (1926), 'The laws of return under competitive conditions', *Economic Journal*, 36, pp. 535-50.

Watson, J. D. (1968), *The Double Helix*, Weidenfeld and Nicolson, London.

Whitaker, J. K. (1990), *Centenary Essays on Alfred Marshall*, Cambridge University Press, Cambridge.

Whitehead, E. A. N. (1987), Letter to *The Times*, 20 January.

Whitley, R. (1984), *The Intellectual and Social Organisation of the Sciences*, Oxford University Press, Oxford.

Williamson, O. E. (1964), *Economics of Discretionary Behavior: Managerial Objectives in a Theory of the Firm*, Prentice-Hall, Englewood Cliffs, NJ.

Williamson, O. E. (1967), 'Hierarchical control and optimum firmsize', *Journal of Political Economy*, 75, pp. 123-38. Reprinted in Williamson (1986), pp. 32-53.

Williamson, O. E. (1981), 'The modern corporation: origin, evolution, attributes', *Journal of Economic Literature*, XIX, pp. 1537-68. Reprinted in Williamson (1986), pp. 131-73.

Williamson, O. E. (1985), *The Economic Institutions of Capitalism*, Free Press, New York.

Williamson, O. E. (1986), *Economic Organization: Firms, Markets and Policy Controls*, Wheatsheaf, Brighton.

Winch, D. M. (1971), *Analytical Welfare Economics*, Penguin, Harmondsworth.

Ziman, J. M. (1978), *Reliable Knowledge*, Cambridge University Press, Cambridge.

Name index

Subject index